America's Next Qua[rterback]
TONY ROMO

TRIUMPH
BOOKS

Written by Mac Engel

To my parents, Ted and Ann Engel
Thanks for your love, support and considerable patience.

Copyright © 2007 by Triumph Books

Photo Editors: Ben Noey Jr. and Mark Rogers

Content packaged by Mojo Media, Inc.
Editor: Joe Funk
Creative Director: Jason Hinman

This book is available in quantity at special discounts for your group or organization.
For further information, contact:

Triumph Books
542 South Dearborn Street
Suite 750
Chicago, IL 60605
Phone: (312) 939-3330
Fax: (312) 663-3557

Printed in the United States of America
ISBN: 978-1-60078-111-7

AP/Wide World

Contents

Prologue

A star is born in the in the Lone Star State

When told that a publishing company was interested in writing a book about Tony Romo, the quarterback of the Dallas Cowboys was surprised. "A book? About me? I'm too young for a book," Romo said.

The only aspect more preposterous than a Tony Romo book, I thought, was that I would be the one to write it. I am the genius who once penned the line for the *Fort Worth Star-Telegram* in August of 2007 that "... no one knows exactly what (Romo is) going to do with the ball when he does something other than hand it off."

I never thought Tony Romo would be where he is today. How could so many team executives, scouts, coaches be so wrong? It doesn't make any sense. It was inconceivable that all 32 NFL teams would pass on a quarterback seven times each such as happened in the 2003 draft, or that he would be anything more than a backup.

This is a league that celebrates doing homework, preparation, studying, etc. This is a league whose coaches make six figures to find and draft players such as Romo, and not ignore them. But this is also a league that screws up, and misses. It is a league where just because someone spends a few million dollars on Player X there is no guarantee of a return on the investment. It's also a league about instant results, and developmental time is measured in weeks.

OK, so some guys fall through the cracks. Patriots quarterback Tom Brady was one of those. But Tom Brady played big time college football at Michigan. We have all heard the argument that Joe Montana fell through the cracks. But he played at Notre Dame. If a guy plays at a Division I-AA school and no one picks him in the draft, he is not going to be a star. If a guy plays at a Division I-AA school and no one picks him in the draft, he's lucky to have a job in the NFL.

But here is Tony Romo, in Dallas, and the quarterback of America's Team.

There may not be a greater or more inspirational story in the NFL today than Romo. No, he didn't come from a dirt-poor environment. There were no tragic tales of death, divorce and his dog didn't run away when he was a kid. He is the nice kid from a small Wisconsin town with the nice parents. His life is from a different era. His life, much like his hometown, reeks of modesty. It reeks of the Midwest. Of 1955.

He wasn't one of these engineered kids from a young age who was raised to play professional sports. Romo didn't play on traveling teams. He was never on the latest Blue Chip whatever list as the most recruited athletes. Colleges or media outlets didn't call him daily to see where he was going to attend college. There was no press conference when he signed his letter of intent to attend a Division I-AA school. There was no press conference to announce much of anything he did for a long time.

Tony Romo's greatest obstacle was to overcome obscurity, and to beat out the perceptions about his height, weight, speed, background, and then to show he was better than the over-hyped guy in front of him.

For every high school athlete who dreams of earning a scholarship, there is Romo to remind them that just because no one notices you doesn't mean you can't earn a scholarship and play collegiate sports. For every college player who dreams of a shot of playing professional football, there is Romo to remind them that it can happen. He is "Hoosiers" – the kid from the small school who represents all of the other kids from the small schools who may never get their shot.

It took a while, but he did it.

From that first snap in the second half against the New York Giants on Monday Night Football in October of 2006 to today, he has done it. Despite the considerable doubt the NFL (and myself) had, all Romo has done is play better than the guy in front of him on every level, and is one of the top quarterbacks in the league.

In the process, he alone has energized one of the biggest fan bases of any professional sports franchise in the world.

For as much money as Cowboys owner Jerry Jones poured into his team, and specifically the quarterback position, since Troy Aikman retired after the 2000 season, they never had The Man. And this league is about The Man at quarterback. Save for the Trent Dilfer, teams don't win the Super Bowl without The Man under center.

But the Cowboys never had The Man, or The Link. The Link to the franchise's proud and distinguished list of quarterbacks – Don Meredith, to Craig Morton, to Roger Staubach, to Danny White to Troy Aikman.

The Cowboys weren't going to win again until they found their link to their storied past. Tony Romo is The Link for the Cowboys.

This is his story and if I didn't write it, I'm not sure I would have believed half of it. ■

Star Light!

In a 21st century fairytale, Tony Romo came out of nowhere to shine

"Romo ... you're in."

Those three innocuous words from Dallas Cowboys quarterbacks coach Chris Palmer launched Tony Romo's professional football career, or the career that people would care about. Until that specific moment inside the Cowboys' locker room inside Texas Stadium during halftime of a Monday Night Football game against the New York Giants on October 23, 2006, Tony Romo was mostly a piece of football curiosity. He was simply the backup.

"You're excited. You don't know if you're going to do any good, but you're just excited," Romo said.

At that point, Tony Romo's best attribute was that the back of his jersey didn't read BLEDSOE ... as in Drew, the suddenly passe starter. The rest? Well, no one really knew for sure.

Romo's promotion wasn't an act of desperation by an aging Hall of Fame head coach whose time on the sidelines was nearing its conclusion. It was just close, or maybe it actually was.

No one – regardless of what people said later – had a clue what Tony Romo would do. No one could say he would become the next franchise quarterback for a team that was is synonymous with them. At that point of that game, Cowboys fans, the coaching staff and the organization just hoped Tony Romo could lead his team back from a 12-7 halftime hole against a division opponent and save them from dropping to 3-3.

How could anyone have a clue that an undrafted Division I-AA player from Eastern Illinois would finally be the answer for a franchise that was built around some of the sports most celebrated quarterbacking names – Don Meredith. Roger Staubach. Troy Aikman.

And after Romo's first throw as "the starter," the future looked as bleak as the recent past, and most recent pass. The play was exciting – he bought time with his feet – moved up in the pocket and threw a

(opposite) Tony Romo's star has risen as fast as any in recent memory.

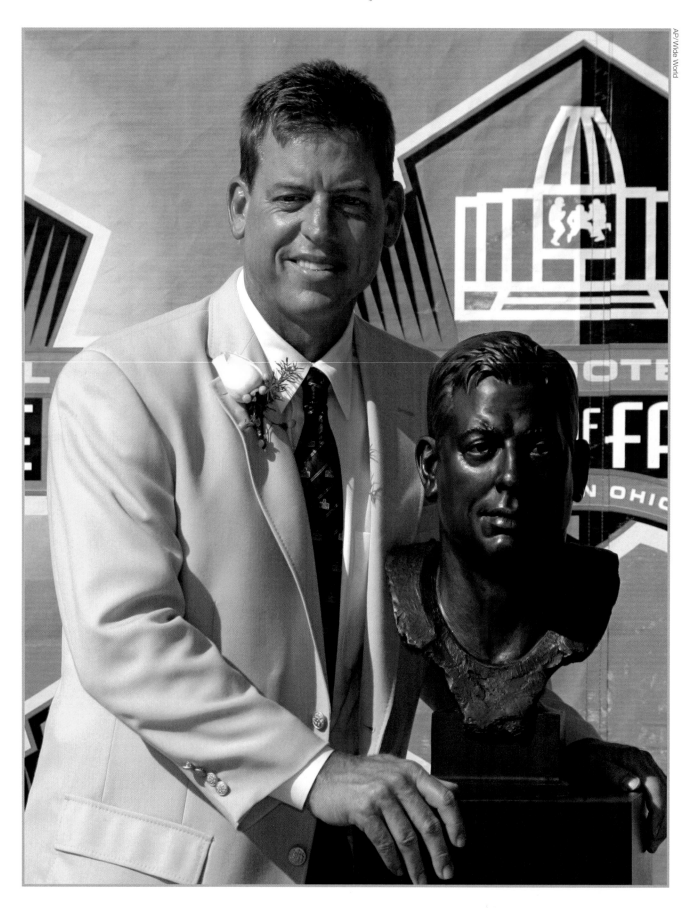

pass intended for rookie tight end Anthony Fasano over the middle. But Romo didn't see Giants linebacker Antonio Pierce floating underneath. Romo's first pass as "The Man" was an interception.

When Romo entered the game on October 23, 2006 he officially became another effort by the Cowboys to find the link to Troy Aikman. Since Aikman retired after the 2000 because of a bad back, concussions and other various injuries, the NFL's most visible, celebrated and often loathed franchise spun rudderless looking for his replacement.

Between the time Aikman retired and the time Romo took the field, this is what Cowboys owner/president/general manager and his team did to find the next Franchise Quarterback.

Jones signed veteran Tony Banks in the 2001 offseason. That move was met with *Fort Worth Star-Telegram* columnist Randy Galloway penning the memorable line: "Losers sign loser."

(Romo was in college at the time.)

Jones selected Georgia quarterback Quincy Carter in the second round of the 2001 draft. Forget the fact that Carter was already benched at Georgia, Jones loved Carter's athletic ability. He saw him as part of the new NFL run/throw quarterback. The Eagles had the prototype in Donovan McNabb. The Cowboys thought Carter could be of that ilk.

The Cowboys cut Banks before the start of the 2001 season, and named Carter as the Opening Day starter under first-year coach Dave Campo. Carter

became the third rookie to start at quarterback for the Cowboys – the others were Aikman and Staubach. Unfortunately, the comparisons stop there. In the season-opening 10-6 loss against the Buccaneers, Carter completed 9-of-19 passes for 34 yards, was sacked twice, intercepted twice and finished with a quarterback rating of 14.5.

That same year, the Cowboys started veteran Anthony Wright, former No. 2 overall pick Ryan Leaf and former Arkansas star Clint Stoerner. Romo was a junior at Eastern Illinois at the time.

The team also signed former Stanford quarterback and St. Louis Cardinals minor league pitcher Chad Hutchinson. He eventually replaced Carter as the starter a little more than midway through the 2002 season. Then offensive coordinator Bruce Coslet said of Hutchinson that the team "hit on this kid." He projected Hutchinson's spot in the Pro Bowl in three years.

A few days after the 2003 NFL draft, they signed Tony Romo to a rookie free agent contract.

In the 2004 offseason, the team made a trade with the Houston Texans to sign former Michigan star and ex-New York Yankees prospect, Drew Henson.

That same offseason, the team signed veteran and Parcells' favorite, 41-year-old Vinny Testaverde. When Testaverde was the No. 1 draft pick in 1987, Romo was process of turning 7.

In the early stages of training camp in 2004, the team released Carter. Parcells later said it was the

(opposite) Since Troy Aikman retired in 2000, the Cowboys had been looking for The Man at quarterback.

toughest cut of his tenure with the Cowboys, mostly because of the time the franchise invested in developing Carter. Some of the things the scouts warned Jones about Carter – primarily the drug use – proved to be sadly correct. He was arrested twice within the span of 10 months, in December of 2006 and October of 2007, for drug possession.

The team signed 33-year-old Drew Bledsoe to be the starter in 2005. Bledsoe was looking to reclaim his status as one of the game's top passers when he signed with the Cowboys. They turned out to be his third, and final, team. When Bledsoe was the No. 1 pick of the 1993 draft out of Washington State, Tony Romo was 13.

In short, the Dallas Cowboys were burning in Quarterback Hell.

Never before in the history of the franchise had the team gone so long, searched so hard and invested so much money and game time to stabilize the most important position on the field. By the time Romo entered the Giants' game, the quarterback position of "America's Team" had been devalued. It didn't mean as much as it once did to be the Cowboys signal caller. It wasn't as if the Cowboys just had bad

(opposite) Bill Parcells had been charged with leading America's Team back to the promised land. (above) Dallas would turn out to be Drew Bledsoe's last NFL stop.

timing with any of those players; they couldn't play or were past their prime.

For all of his efforts, all Jerry Jones got was a multi-million dollar migraine. The Cowboys had had some low points at the position before in their history – do the names Steve Pelluer or Gary Hogeboom mean anything? – but nothing like this. "As long as I was there we never went through a period like that," said former Cowboys director of scouting, Gil Brandt, who started with the team with Tom Landry and Tex Schramm. "I was with Tex in Los Angeles, and he was a big believer in quarterbacks. So we always brought them in, and Tom developed them."

Under Brandt, Schramm and Landry, the Cowboys were about the quarterback. They began with Don Meredith, who before he became an icon as the foil to Howard Cossell on Monday Night Football, led the Cowboys to the NFL Championship game in 1966, the same year he was named the league's player of the year.

Then there was Craig Morton, no slouch, either, before "Captain America" Roger Staubach took over and became the face of the Cowboys in the prosperous days of the 1970s. All these years later, Staubach remains an icon to the Cowboys, their fans and Texas residents.

The "worst" it had truly been was Danny White, who replaced Staubach, "and Danny led us to three consecutive NFC championship games," Brandt

noted. White was no bum. He just never won a Super Bowl.

Then came Troy Aikman, and those three Super Bowls.

In the offseason of Aikman's retirement, Jones made finding his replacement a priority. He wanted the next Troy.

But Jones resisted the idea of drafting a quarterback high in the draft the way a child does eating a plate full of beets and asparagus. He had done it once with Aikman, the first year he owned the franchise in 1989; but Jones walked into that pick. It was waiting for him when he bought the team. He personally didn't have to suffer through a year to "earn" a spot at the top of the draft.

Three Super Bowls later, Jones had proof that while beets and asparagus might not taste as good as chocolate cake they built Super Bowl muscle. But rebuilding that muscle wasn't easy. To do it using the same method he drafted Aikman meant his would be one of the league's worst. It's not in Jones' nature to throw something away in the name of developing one single player. His zeal to win prevented him from deliberately entering a season that could finish close to his first 1-15 year in 1989. There had to be an easier, or at the very least a less excruciating, way to find the franchise, superstar quarterback.

"I've been trying since Troy, I've been trying to get a quarterback without going to the top of that draft and having to make that commitment and the

(opposite) Cowboys owner Jerry Jones had been looking for success, but seemingly no quarterback option worked.

consequences of missing with that kind of commitment," Jones said in October of 2006. "I've been trying to do that. Now I may have ended up paying the same price over a period of time but I have consciously tried not to go to the top of the draft to get a QB. And that's been a plan. I did it with Quincy and that's why when Chad was available, that's why those guys...that's why I've done it, the way I've done it. Because I've seen the damage that can happen when you go to the top of that draft, make the kind of commitments that you make with your cap for the future – can't avoid them when you get up

there – and bet it all right there. And I've seen how other clubs have done it. It was a different time."

By the time Aikman retired, other teams had demonstrated that your favorite team didn't have to bottom out, draft the quarterback with a top five pick, and struggle again before winning.

Other teams were winning Super Bowls with the new "bus driver" quarterbacks that were popping up all over the league. They were the guys who didn't get in the way. Their teams called them "excellent game managers." They didn't make plays, but their forte was not screwing up. They were usually less

(opposite) Quincy Carter showed promise, but his NFL career would be derailed by arrests and legal problems.
(above) America's Team was looking for America's Quarterback, and that certainly wasn't Chad Hutchinson.

expensive than a first round pick, and a castoff from somewhere else. And, every now and then, they also worked.

Teams such as the Cowboys looked at the Buccaneers with evny when former seventh round pick Brad Johnson leding them to their first-ever Super Bowl title in 2002. Jones watched the Baltimore Ravens win their first Super Bowl with Trent Dilfer – yes, that Trent Dilfer – as their quarterback in 2000. This was the same Dilfer the Buccaneers selected with the sixth pick in the 1993 draft. They dumped him after the '99 season. The Ravens picked him up, and all he had to do was get out of the way - he threw 12 touchdowns and 11 interceptions in 2000 with the Ravens. Yet they won the Super Bowl, mostly because their defense was one of the best ever.

So it could be done. Thanks to the salary cap, and free agency, and teams going from 3-13 to 13-3 in a year, maybe Jones didn't need to throw a season in the garbage can all in the name of drafting a top quarterback, and then, after said quarterback was picked, waste another year developing said top quarterback. All in the hopes of the top quarterback panning out, and not developing into another Ryan Leaf. The name continues to embody the concept of the BUST.

And it scared the hell out of Jones. Leaf was the second pick in the 1998 draft, or one behind Peyton Manning. The Chargers had dealt two first round picks, a second round picks, a reserve linebacker and Pro Bowl running back Eric Metcalf to the Cardinals to move up to select Leaf. Leaf was a complete bust, and out of football by 2002.

If there had been a guarantee of another three Super Bowls, Jones might have swallowed another plate full of asparagus and beets, or 1-15. Aikman took a beating his rookie year, but in the words of the gym teachers and old Jesuits everywhere, the drubbings had built character. Aikman developed into one of the best passers and leaders the sport had. He has the bust in the Pro Football Hall of Fame to prove his worth. And the Cowboys went on to be the team of the 1990s. With Aikman passing the ball to Michael Irvin, Jay Noveck or Alvin Harper, and handing the ball to Emmitt Smith, the Cowboys reclaimed their spot as one of the world's most recognized and successful sports franchises.

But every dynasty fades, or dies. A free agent loss here. A retirement there. A drug problem here. An arrest there. By the time 2000 came, Aikman was fighting injuries, not to mention a roster short on young talent. His retirement triggered a collapse at the quarterback position that Dallas had never seen before in the history of one of the league's most distinguished franchises.

America's Team no longer featured America's Quarterback. Players such as Peyton Manning, Brett Favre or Tom Brady were America's Quarterbacks.

When Romo entered the game that October

(opposite) The Cowboys and their fans longed for the glory days of Aikman, Emmitt Smith, and Michael Irvin and were hoping to find it in the early 2000s.

Of the 2003 quarterbacking corps of Hutchinson, Carter, Romo and Clint Stoerner (pictured left to right), Romo is the only one still in the NFL.

night, he became the 10th quarterback to play for the Cowboys since 2001. Before he entered the game, America's Team was 38-47 in that time, and Jones had spent millions of dollars in an attempt to find his quarterback. And no matter what coach Bill Parcells or Jones said, the idea of starting Romo at all in 2006 meant something had gone terribly awry. Either Bledsoe was injured, or the white flag had been raised. This was a team that sold Super Bowl as a realistic possibility. Undrafted quarterbacks who had never played a meaningful NFL snap don't lead teams to Super Bowls.

"I did not want to this year go to an inexperienced quarterback. I wanted to have the benefit of Drew Bledsoe," Jones said two days after Bledsoe was benched. "I knew when we started the season that if we went away from Drew Bledsoe that meant we were facing some challenges that I didn't want to face during the season. My picture of us having a lot of success this year has to do with Drew having a top year.

"We didn't want to take that risk (of playing a young quarterback). I was not for taking that risk early because we thought of what we could possibly be with Bledsoe and our offense being about where we were at this time last year with how he was playing and how we were playing at that position.

"I have to be a realist. If we are making this adjustment right now I hadn't thought or hoped that we'd be sitting here after the sixth game making these adjustments. This change. But I'm not in any way thinking with the amount of games that we have left with the team we have with the plusses that Tony could bring to us I'm not in any way dismissing the possibilities this year."

Jones equated during training camp that to play Romo meant they were essentially playing a rookie at the most crucial position on the field. Technically, Romo had been in the NFL for four seasons. As it would later prove to be cruelly ironic, until he was considered a legitimate prospect the only way Romo made his way onto an NFL field was as the holder on field goals and extra points. Jones saw Romo as a rookie quarterback. And if Troy Aikman couldn't win as a rookie quarterback, and neither could John Elway, Peyton Manning or countless other celebrated names, then how could an undrafted player from a school in Charleston, Illinois be expected to immediately come in and "save a season"?

There was a curious optimism when Romo trotted out to start the second half. At that point, the team wanted him in. Several players had gone to Parcells in the previous weeks to lobby for Romo. Bledsoe had lost the team. "It's the newest pretty girl," Parcells said of any Romo/Bledsoe controversy the week of the 2006 season opener. "It's just like the actresses in Hollywood. It's the new pretty face. 'Oh we like that better than we like that one. Oh, we like this next one.'"

After Antonio Pierce intercepted Romo, the

AP/Wide World

"next pretty face" looked a lot like the last one. By the end of that night, Romo threw two more interceptions, one of which was returned for a touchdown. He had shown the ability to move around the pocket, and he could make a few plays with his feet. He completed 14-of-25 passes for 227 yards with two touchdowns and three interceptions. The Giants won, 36-22. He told Jones he'd never make those mistakes again. The Cowboys dropped to 3-3. None of the players knew the next day which quarterback would start.

"I don't feel very good about the situation right now," Romo said after the game. "I definitely would have liked to have performed better. Hopefully next week that will change."

But after the game no one knew if Romo would have a next week. As an undrafted player, he was not going to receive the luxury that a first round pick would. By NFL standards, the Cowboys hadn't invested much in Romo, so they could part ways with him much easier than a first round pick. After all, Romo wasn't even a draft pick in any round.

In the end, Romo gave the Dallas Cowboys the link to the past they had so desperately sought. ■

(above) In his early appearances Romo did not impress Cowboys owner Jerry Jones, but Romo would soon prove that he belonged in the NFL.

Thriving In Anonymity

Not such a long way from Dairyland to big D

Tony Romo was really late. So late the 23-year-old head coach was forced to think about leaving without his starting sophomore point guard. Steve Brezowitz was a first- year boys' basketball coach at Burlington High School; he wanted to lay down the law to his players, and waiting a few more minutes past the We're Leaving Without You mark for Tony Romo would look like exactly what it was – preferential treatment.

But Brezowitz was no fool and, despite his inexperience as a basketball coach, he knew the universal truth of coaching: To win on the road, you need your best player, especially when it's against one your bigger rivals, in this case East Troy. "We really need him," Brezowitz told his assistant coach. He called the Romo residence. No answer. Cell phones were not ubiquitous then. There were only so many phones Brezowitz could call.

He had to get his team moving; it was already snowing hard. He had waited an extra five minutes

for Romo, which felt like five months. What he didn't know was that Romo was on his way to East Troy, too ... on his bicycle, in the snow. Romo's father, Ramiro, always gave his son a ride to whatever game he was scheduled to play. But he Ramiro was out of town and late because of the snow. So Tony improvised. Fortunately, his father saw him en route and picked him for a straight drive to East Troy.

"There was this rule that you had to ride the bus to play," Brezowitz said. But these were extenuating circumstances. An exception was made. "We would have been dead without him," Brezowitz said. "We won in overtime."

Tony Romo was born in San Diego to Joan and Ramiro Romo in 1980. Tony was the youngest of three – he had older sisters Danielle and Jossalyn.

Two years later, the Romo's moved to the quiet area of Burlington, Wisconsin, population 10,000 ... give or take a few suburbanites. Located about

(opposite) Romo, pictured here in college, played his college football at Eastern Illinois University after growing up in southeastern Wisconsin.

30 miles south of Milwaukee, Burlington has the feel of a small town that the developers can't wait to get their hands on.

Look hard enough and it would be easy to see a Norman Rockwell scene. It has a quaint town square, complete with a few chocolate shops, one blinking red light, and a movie theatre. Not until you reach the outskirts of Burlington do you see chain establishments such as a Wendys or other fast food places. Everything else is unique to Burlington – Napoli's Italian restaurant, Coach's Sports Bar and Grill, And Fred's, Home of the World Famous Burgers. And when the wind blows just right, you can easily sweet smell of chocolate that eminates from the Nestle's Chocolate factory in town, and helped give Burlington the nickname, "Chocolate City, USA."

This is where Ramiro and Joan wanted to raise their family after he finished his tour with the Navy. This is where Tony Romo grew up.

Romo grew up in the same 1,000-square foot house his parents live in today. His father took the family back to Burlington in 1982 when he entered the construction business, and the house has his handiwork all over it. They wanted this type of town and community to raise their children. And Ramiro was and remains very much the head of his house. "Romo is very strict," Joan said.

She calls her husband Romo. Her son is Tony.

Ramiro and Joan didn't raise Tony to be the next quarterback of America's Team. He didn't drink protein shakes as a kid. He wasn't on some super workout program. He led the typical Midwestern existence. Tony went to church on Sundays. He participated in the Christmas nativity scene, sometimes as the shepherd. He enjoyed Sunday school. His mother and family insisted that even as their children grew older that the family eat together five nights a week.

He wasn't much for mischief. About the closest he got into trouble was in the first grade when a teacher called Joan – turns out his sister had forged Joan's signature for something. Or the time he found his sister Danielle's diary when he was a teenager, "And that nearly started World War III," Joan said. There was the time when rain prevented the normal recess period. He taught whoever was interested how to make the triangular paper football, which led to bit of a mess at school. "It was always little things," Joan said.

Tony did not have the conventional teenage job, either. He had but a few summer jobs – worked at a hospital once. That didn't last long. Worked at a restaurant once, and that didn't last long, either.

Nor was Tony exactly what one might call a nerd. "Tony Romo, sophomore, power mechanics, Row 3, Seat 2," said one of his high school teachers, Bob Musgrave. "Always thought he was paying attention when he got there early. We sat at this bench on stools and he's looking at his knees. I

(opposite) In the offseason, Romo runs a football camp in his hometown of Burlington, Wisconsin.

thought he was paying attention. Little did I know had he swiped the sports section from my table and was reading it during the class. He didn't care much for the classroom. But he was good enough."

Tony's passions were sports, sports, sports and sports. Not necessarily in that order, either. He loved to win. Joan isn't so sure that Tony didn't take the Monopoly money from the neighbor's house to ensure that he'd win in games at the house. When Ramiro came home one afternoon when Tony was a teenager, he asked his son to move some materials and supplies to the back of the house. "It was Tony's job, but that was work and I would help and we made it into an exercise - How many boards can you move?" one of his childhood friends, Paul Bendar, said. "You have to move a bunch of wood, which stinks. But we made it into a competition, an exercise, a workout. All the things kids don't want to do, we made it into a competition." The two would order a pizza and play chess for hours in the Romo's basement.

As a kid, Tony played everything he could. Soccer. Baseball. Football. Basketball. Tennis. Golf.

Baseball didn't take. He wanted to be a pitcher, but accuracy was lacking. "He just didn't know where the ball was going," Ramiro said. "But as a catcher, he was accurate as hell."

Tennis was more of a high school diversion. "As a ninth grader the tennis coach was in my department and Tony was goofing around playing the

No. 3 varsity singles player," his high school golf coach, Bill Berkholtz, said. "He picked it up. He was playing the guy in a pickup game and he just crushed him."

Tony wanted to play both. But golf won out, probably because his dad played. It went golf, basketball, then football. In that order.

Tony began playing golf when he was eight or nine. He'd go with his dad. Ramiro would take a shot and, wherever tee shot landed, is where Tony teed up. His mother worked at the local golf course, so often times Tony could be found running around the course there. "I could think of about 1,000 things I'd rather do than play golf," she said. She was in the minority. Her daughter Jocelyn was on the golf team, too. The golf course became a miniature day center at times. It's the golf game that nearly every coach who has worked with Romo credits his ability as a quarterback. Golf is entirely about the next shot, about looking ahead. There is no lamenting.

"He was so patient on the golf course," Berkholtz said. "When he throws an interception, it's a golfer mentality; make a bad shot let it fester or you can say that's done its on to the next shot. I really think that he had he devoted just everything to golf he could have made it as a professional golfer."

One sport? Nonsense. This was a kid who once asked for a set of bases as a Christmas present.

(opposite) An all-around athlete, Romo is also an excellent golfer.

Tony was about playing every sport thing he could. And getting himself completely immersed in football and basketball. His mother has told the story umpteen million times about the time Tony watched the VHS tape on former NBA legend Pistol "Pete" Maravich so much he burned it out. Three times. Tony personally went through VCRs the way a dog does a chew toy.

When the family added a basketball hoop to their driveway, Ramiro looked at it and thought there was no way Tony could make a basket. He was five or six, and too short to make shots on a regulation 10-foot goal. They never lowered the basket, though. And when it snowed, Tony would shovel a square around the basket so he could shoot. "The little guy would be out there for two hours and make two baskets," Ramiro said.

When Tony wasn't playing ball, he'd be in the basement watching movies. He watched the unbelievably corny "The Program" to the point where he memorized every single line. The same with the Robert Redford film, "The Natural". His parents would buy he and his friends pizzas, mostly because by doing so they'd be able to keep an eye on their son. They weren't big on video games, so if Tony wanted to play those he'd have to do it at a friend's house. Rather than go out on Friday nights, Tony often stayed in with friends and watched movies.

Tony also powered through sports books — one in particular about Larry Bird struck a chord. When Tony watched football games he didn't focus on the highlight hit or long touchdown pass. He watched the mechanics of the players. When something struck him, he'd write it down on his notepad that usually was by his bed. Notes that would read: "Keep your eye on the ball" or "Keep your head down".

Eventually, all of those little notes would serve Tony well.

The new high school was built a few miles away, and it has a more modern football stadium and basketball gym. Dinty Moore Stadium is no longer the home for the Burlington Demons high school football team. Where Tony Romo played his high school football and basketball still has a 1950s feel. The smell from the chocolate factory hangs in the air around the field.

The decaying field itself wasn't big enough to host a high school playoff game. The black gravel track that circles the field cuts through the corners of the end zones. Hardly the big time, but this is where Romo became a quarterback.

He started as a sophomore, and the Demons finished 9-3 that season. All the things that Romo made famous in the NFL - the improvising - began here, on these fields.

"There was one time this kid had him sacked, and he changed hands with the ball and threw it left handed 20 yards," his high school coach, Steve

(opposite) Growing up, Romo admired Pistol Pete Maravich so much that he managed to wear out a tape of his highlights.

Gerber, said. "He was so damn smart. When you see guys splash off of him he was capable of doing that on the edge. He would make such good decisions."

Or at least most of the time. By the time Romo was a senior, he badly wanted to play on defense. Make a hit. Maybe he'd intercept a pass. Something on defense. Unbeknownst to his coach, towards the end of one game, Romo put himself in as the team's safety. He screamed on his way on to the field "Starting defense, baby!" It was a line straight from "The Program". Tony didn't make it one play. The coach figured out why his defense looked unfamiliar and took his star quarterback out before the ball was snapped.

Romo went into the huddle near the end of game, dropped to a knee and looked at his teammates. "OK, let's the put the women and children to bed and go looking for dinner!" he said. Again, straight from "The Program".

"You still see that today," high school teammate, Steve Tenhagen, said. "He always screwed around like that. Guys loved that. He's ultra competitive, but can still keep a sense of humor about what he's doing."

Tony is corny, but it's extremely sincere. This was a kid who as an eighth grader wrote on a football, "I play for the love of the game." Who does that? Tony Romo.

Wisconsin high school re-classified before the start of Romo's junior year. They became one of the smallest high schools in the biggest classification. The team was pretty good, but they were overmatched. It didn't help that Romo wasn't very big - maybe 6-feet, and skinny. His team was losing. No one from the college ranks much noticed Tony Romo, the football player.

Now Tony Romo the basketball player? He got noticed a little more. Tony played basketball all of the time. He would go to the high school gym before school to play with the adults. He was told to stop; no matter, he adjusted and would drive in the mornings to play at a different school.

But his coach, Steve Brezowitz, was a little frustrated by Tony early on. OK, a lot frustrated. Tony didn't work too hard at it. He didn't have to because he was very good; very good as in better than anyone else on his team, and that was enough. It wasn't until his father talked to Tony as a teenager when good enough became not enough.

"God gave you something," Ramiro told his son. "If you don't want to take it any further, that's fine. We're going to love you no matter what. But take that gift you still have to work at it. We're not going to tell you to do this. And we're not going to make you do it."

By the time Tony was a senior, he had become one of the best players in the area. But his size hurt him. And Tony was not an athlete who ran around looking to play on AAU basketball teams, or some other high profile traveling team that is a de-facto

(opposite) Romo has come a long way from being the quarterback of his high school team, the Burlington Demons.

minor league for the colleges. Tony never even attended football camps. Ramiro freely admits he didn't know much about those sorts of things.

He was invited to attend one at Notre Dame in the spring of his junior year, but he had already spent money on prom, he'd asked a girl, so he didn't go to the camp.

Tony was a throwback. He wasn't a one-sport star whose life focus was just basketball. Or just football. Or just baseball. By the time Romo was playing, the popularity of dedicating your time to one sport year-round as a teen had grown. Tony preferred to play everything; the change in season meant a change in the game he played.

There is an unmistakable pride throughgout Burlington in Tony's success.

Fred's Hamburgers has a table dedicated to Romo; pictures, stats, etc. The sports bar was selling "Viva Romo" sweatshirts when Romomania swept through the NFL in 2006. His grade school put up a sign congratulating him. And Romo still returns home every summer to host a football camp.

This town is by no means some crumbling, dying vision of small town America. It will be a suburb of Milwaukee in 10 years. The Wal-Mart that sits on the edge of town is a sign of what is coming. But Tony is before that. He came from Burlington before the new high school was built. Before the new, big subdivision of houses was built on the west side of town. And he is beloved there.

"A few years ago, I was divorced after 19 years," his high school football coach, Steve Gerber, said. "And it was Christmas time. My son Eric was 11 at the time, and we go over to visit Tony at his house. I bring a six pack of beer; anybody who has been through divorce you feel for your kids and how they're doing. I took Eric along. He had family over and lots of family. Kids running all over the place. We sit down at the kitchen table and it's a very blue-collar family. We're talking football with, Joan, Tony and Tony's dad. There are kids running through your legs. He's telling me about Dallas and he says, 'Coach, I'll be right back.' He goes down to the basement and comes up, and he pulls out from behind his back a game jersey and he gives it to Eric."

"Tony said, 'This is a Christmas present. I think he was perceptive of a lot of things. For him to do that that day, it made me feel so special. My son doesn't wear the jersey. He takes the jersey to my place or his mom's. He said dad, 'You can wear it when you go down there to the game in Dallas.' That memory of Tony is probably the most special one I have."

By the time Tony Romo was a senior the collective Division I football and basketball world had no clue who he was, and didn't have much interest in finding out. He was too short. Too skinny. Too slow. Nothing jumped out future Dallas Cowboys quarterback. If anything jumped out it was the idea that maybe Tony would play football and basketball at Wisconsin-Whitewater, a Division III school not too far from Burlington.

By the late fall of 1997, Eastern Illinois offensive coordinator Roy Wittke began receiving some information from some very reliable people that Burlington had a pretty good athlete playing quarterback and running point guard. Wittke was raised in Racine, Wisconsin, and his parents mailed him an article from the Racine newspaper about Tony Romo.

Wittke decided he'd be the first to look. He saw some game film of Romo playing quarterback his senior season against Oak Creek, a suburb of Milwaukee, and a perennial power. "What stood out about that game was that Tony threw for something like 300 or 400 yards against a really good team," Wittke said. Wittke wasn't sold, however, until he went to Burlington to watch Romo play a basketball game. Then he thought Romo had a shot. The head coach wasn't so sure and preferred not to recruit Romo.

"I have to admit it, I really didn't think he could do anything. Coach Wittke was the guy who had to convince me," Eastern Illinois football coach Bob Spoo said. "He is the one who deserves the credit on him." Wittke is the one who put Romo at I-AA Eastern Illinois.

Division I-AA football is another world away from Division I. The stadiums seat modest capaci-

ties, usually somewhere in the area of 10,000 to 15,000, rather than the 100,000-plus seats at Michigan or Tennessee. Eastern Illinois' O'Brien Stadium sits 10,000. The games usually featured the directional schools – Northern Iowa vs. Southeast Missouri State. There are no big TV contracts with ESPN exist. The athletic department budgets are of the shoe string variety. Teams takes buses to road games. No four-star accomodations on road trips. This is what awaited Tony Romo ... maybe.

Romo came for an official visit to Charleston, Illinois in January of 1998. The night after dinner, Wittke compiled a quick highlight tape to show to Coach Spoo. He would show the coach the tape before he met with Romo. "I know why Coach Spoo resisted him – because Tony was raw. I don't want to say 'project' but, Coach Spoo was a quarterback guy. He had been around good ones from his days at Purdue, and he was skeptical.

"What was readily apparent was that Tony was a gym rat. He was a serious competitor. He played several sports. He was an overall athlete - that was what I tried to sell Coach Spoo," Wittke said. "What it came down to was I felt Tony had a good frame, and he would get bigger and stronger and was worth the risk of a partial scholarship."

Partial scholarship. Partial. Partials are handed out in college baseball, volleyball, swimming, track, not football. Football players receive full

scholarships. NFL quarterbacks are not only drafted, but they don't pay for college. Ever.

"I think a partial scholarship at that time was probably worth between $4,000 and $5,000," Spoo said. This was the only college scholarship offer the future quarterback of the Dallas Cowboys would receive. So Tony took it.

In that same recruiting class was a quarterback named Julius Davis. He had a full scholarship. On paper, Davis probably should have been in Division I football somewhere. Maybe at Illinois, or at least Western Michigan. Davis was from Chicago; listed 5-foot-10, 170 pounds, he was expected to be the Panthers' quarterback in the next year or so. He was more of the mold of an Eastern Illinois quarterback - fast, agile, quick, and he could throw. The Panthers were a run first, pass second team. Davis fit that description.

Romo redshirted that first season in 1997. Davis as a Prop 48 case. That's an NCAA term for student athletes who are admitted, but don't have every single academic requirement checked off. He had to burn his redshirt years as what was called a "prop" casualty.

Romo didn't much impress his skeptical head coach. "He really didn't have the best arm. And, I think more than anything else, he didn't know what it took just yet in terms of the work or the dedication," Spoo said. There was even some thought maybe Romo would leave.

Romo was not the first athlete to attend college and be a little lost, though. In high school, Romo had been the best athlete on just about every field or court he played on. College was different. He wasn't the best any more, not automatically. "Once he figured that out, then you really started to see what this kid could do," Spoo said. "He'd always stay after practice. Throwing extra. Preparing. As a coach, you loved him."

As a redshirt freshman, he competed with Davis for the backup job. Romo won it, and appeared in three games that season, most notably a 31-21 loss at Central Florida. The team finished 2-10 that season. The next spring would be Romo's chance. The school that was reluctant to give him a scholarship put him against the guy with the full ride for the starting position. "It wasn't even close," Wittke said of the competition between Romo and Davis.

Romo led the Panthers to consecutive victories, including a 72-0 spanking of Kentucky Wesleyan, to begin his sophomore year. By season's end, Romo had led Eastern Illinois to its first I-AA playoff appearance since 1996. They lost to top-ranked Montana, 45-13. Romo passed for 2,583 yards and 27 touchdowns that season — and this was a running offense — and was named the Ohio Valley Conference Player of the Year.

A lot had changed, Romo was bigger, A little more serious. But one thing didn't change. After every game, Tony would spend time talking to his

(opposite) Among the accolades Romo won at Eastern Illinois was the Walter Payton Award, given annually to the nation's best I-AA football player.

parents about the game. They were almost always at every game their son played. "They would talk for at least an hour," Joan said. "I never really liked football. But Tony would teach me things about it. And he'd ask, 'Did you notice I did this or that? I did that for you.'"

His junior year was more of the same, only better. Both Spoo and Wittke feared their star quarterback may have peaked. "You see with kids that come of nowhere they just plateau and they never really get any better," Wittke said. "That was never the case with Tony. He just always kept improving."

He never stopped playing. When the team bus would stop for a break at a rest area or restaurant, Romo would grab a football and throw with his teammates in the parking lot. What Spoo and Wittke loved about Romo then is the same characteristic his current coaches love about him as a pro: He just wants to win. There was no fascination with his own statistics, which were gaudy. Romo didn't chart his own personal anything. If his team won and he passed for zero yards, fine, great. Romo was happy.

There was one game in particular in Romo's junior year, that it probably could have been. It was Homecoming week at Eastern Illinois, and a bus-load of family and friends drove from Burlington to see the Panthers play Southeast Missouri. Unfortunately, a rain storm hit. And not just any rain – monsoon conditions.

All of those family and friends who traveled to watch their hometown boy slice up the air were crushed. Tony Romo didn't attempt one single pass that day. Near the end of the game, as the Panthers drained the clock, Romo came over to the sidelines and put on the headset to talk to his coaches, "One of these runs here I'm going to run a naked bootleg just to get my one pass in for today," he said.

He was kidding. The Panthers won 12-0.

"He never said a word about it," Wittke said of Romo's "passing" performance. "He didn't care. We won."

By the end of his junior year, Romo showed the Brett Favre-flair that he had in high school, and is known for in the pros. His flair that coaches and fans collectively say, "No! No! No! ... Yes! Yes! Yes!" Could that flair and improv lead to a negative play or an interception? Yes. Could it lead to a bigger play? Yes. So the coaches lived with it, and evan began to need it.

The Panthers finished 9-2 that season and won the OVC title with a 6-0 mark. The Panthers returned to the playoffs to face Northern Iowa in the first round. Romo passed for 386 yards and five touchdowns, but it wasn't enough. The Panthers lost, 49-43. For the second time in as many years, Romo was named the conference player of the year as he passed for 2,068 yards with 21 touchdowns.

But no one talked much about Tony Romo, even as he entered his senior year. Such is the life of a Division I-AA player. "It's much harder to get noticed at this level," Spoo admitted.

Not that Romo didn't try. But hardly anyone noticed. The team opened with a pair of games against Division I opponents — at Hawaii and at Kansas State. These are called "guarantee" games, because the visiting school is guaranteed a certain amount of money, usually in the few hundred thousand dollar range. And the home school is virtually guaranteed a win. The Panthers were drilled by the combined score of 124-39. "I don't remember playing against him at all," said Cowboys defensive back Terence Newman, who played against Romo in that game in 2002 at Kansas State.

But Romo went on to pass for a career-high 3,165 yards with 34 touchdowns that season, the Panthers finished 8-4 and qualified for the playoffs again. It was during this year, after a game, Romo told his dad, "I think I can play in the NFL."

"Oh, you are huh?" Ramiro said. On the four and a half hour drive from Charleston to Burlington, Ramiro worried. "What am I going to do now with him?" he asked Joan. "I don't know if he can play. I don't know."

Again the Panthers lost in the first round, 48-9, against second-ranked Western Illinois. Romo's last college game was not his best — he was sacked three times, threw one interception was fumbled once.

For the third consecutive year, Romo was named the OVC player of the year. His name was at the top of nearly every major passing category in Eastern Illinois history, usually next to a former EIU alum, Sean Payton. It's a fact that would help Romo greatly in the coming months.

(Whatever happened to that quarterback who Romo was supposed to backup, Julius Davis? By his senior year he was moved to wide receiver and appeared in four games.)

After Romo's senior season was complete, Romo was given the Walter Payton Award, which goes annually to the nation's top I-AA player. The award sits on top of the entertainment center in Romo's home in Burlington. It's the only obvious sign that Romo played football on any level in the house. Most of the other signs are pictures in the basement; all of those trophies, plaques and awards from his days at Burlington and Eastern Illinois are mostly stored in a closet, or in one of the giant Rubbermaid containers in the closet.

"Did I feel he had a chance to be a starting quarterback at Eastern Illinois? Yes I did. That's why we recruited him," Wittke said.

"Now, and I've been asked this 1,000 times: Did I think Tony would be the starting quarterback of the Dallas Cowboys? Not in 100 years."

Try 100 million years. ■

A Sudden Rise

A new sheriff rides into the Cowboys' lineup

The two quarterbacks did not have to wait 100 million years to find out who start the week after the Monday Night defeat against the Giants. It may have just felt like it.

One day after the loss against the Giants, neither Bledsoe nor Romo knew would start the next game, at Carolina. Only the staff knew who would be the starting quarterback for the Cowboys in Week 7 of the 2006 NFL season. The Cowboys were 3-3 at the time, and dream of a Super Bowl run was classified as preposterous, especially if Romo was the quarterback. There was a thought floating around the Cowboys' training facility at Valley Ranch that coach Bill Parcells would return to Bledsoe.

What people didn't know was that at half time of the game against the Giants, Parcells was officially done with Bledsoe.

Bledsoe's interception late in the first half against the Giants caused Parcells to say enough was finally enough. The play was designed to go to the right, not for receiver Terry Glenn who was facing tight "press" coverage from Giants defensive back Sam Madison on the opposite side. Bledsoe threw for Glenn anyway, and Madison easily jumped the route to intercept the pass at the goal line. Parcells liked players to follow their gut, but inside a team's 20-yard line was not the time to freelance. He had been trying for years to bang this into Bledsoe's head. Bledsoe was 35, and Parcells didn't want his quarterback to learn any new tricks as much as he wanted him to drop some bad habits.

He was going with Romo. The decision was made on Tuesday, but Romo didn't find out until Wednesday, the same with the rest of the players. "I knew what I had just done," Parcells said recalling the change. "We were going forward from there. I knew that was what we needed to do. I was ready to find out if this guy was going to work."

He waited until Wednesday morning to tell his

(opposite) While they may have distinctly different personalities off the field, Terrell Owens and Romo have forged a productive relationship on the field.

players. "I loved it," defensive end Chris Canty said. "Whatever was happening, it couldn't be as bad as it was. I'd say it the locker room was split; half with Drew and half with Tony. Drew was a vet. He was an older guy, and maybe he didn't relate as well to the younger players. This was a younger team. And Tony is a younger guy, so he related better to us."

Parcells waited a few more hours to tell the rest of the world. "We're going to start Romo this week," Parcells told the local media matter-of-factly. "I'm happy to answer any questions about that you might have."

Where to begin?

By that point the most Romo had shown was in preseason, practice with the second team offense, handing the ball off at the end of a blowout, and spotting the ball on field goals and extra points. He was the backup – nice, affable, incredibly confident and damn sure he was better than the starter. Romo had shown positives in every preseason he played in. But then again, who cares? To quote the great Allen Iverson, "We're talking about practice."

This was real.

Romo would make his first NFL start on NBC's new toy, Sunday Night Football, against the Panthers in Carolina. The unbridled optimism the Cowboys entered the season with had been evicted by cautious optimism born from a mediocre start. The Cowboys were beginning a three-game road trip: At Carolina, Washington, and Arizona. An 0-3 stint, a realistic scenario with a "rookie quarterback", which pretty much would trash the season.

"This is a much different time, so it's not conjecture, it's not what we think, it's time to go and do it," Parcells said a few days before the game. "Now, I don't expect perfection, but hopefully he'll give us a little something."

Romo's take on it was loaded with the perspective of someone who logic said should not be in this position. If he was good, he was good. If he wasn't, he wasn't. It was, after, just a football game. Nobody died. He believed in himself, some would say arrogantly so, and if he was good enough the rest would take care of itself.

"I'm pretty realistic about my talents and abilities in certain areas," Romo said that week. "I've bullcrapped myself on stuff like that and say, 'I am really good' if I perform poorly. I will do something to fix it because I know that's my weakness. While some people aren't able to see their weakness, I have been able to improve upon those. That's how I don't think you can look at yourself as a career backup or just another guy. As long as you can see improvement in your own game or until you stop improving you always think the sky is the limit. That's how you approach it."

It made for a good sound bite on the local news. Whether or not it would help yield an effective quarterback – who knew?

(opposite) At first, the extent of Romo's workload was limited to practice and warming up before games. His only regular in-game action consisted of holding the ball for the kicker on special teams.

Week 8: At Carolina, November 5, 2006

NBC play by play man Al Michaels gushed about the Cowboys new quarterback, claiming that his candor was a breath of fresh air. In the pre-game interviews with Michaels and John Madden, Romo spelled it all out. His recent breakup with his long-time girlfriend. His love for Packers quarterback Brett Favre. He even did his best Favre throwing impersonation. Romo was indeed a breath of fresh air. He didn't know better than to lie his way through an interview.

This was the first time America, and really Cowboy Nation, were introduced to Tony Romo. At that point, they knew he was 6-foot-2, 225 pounds and didn't fit the physical descriptions of the "great" quarterbacks. This was truly the first time they saw the smile that grates on opponents, but teammates find infectious. The first time they saw his dimple in his left cheek, or the mole on the opposite side. The first time they saw his child-like, playground enthusiasm. He has a bit of goofball in him that teeters on nerdishness.

While this was nice, Romo was still making his first NFL start. And his first drive against the Panthers didn't look much better than the second half against the Giants. On the Cowboys' third offensive play of the night, he was sacked by Panthers defensive lineman Kris Jenkins. But the next series he began to show signs of life and calmer nerves. He led his team into scoring range, but

kicker Mike Vanderjagt promptly banged a 48-yard field goal attempt off the right upright.

So the Cowboys were trailing 7-0 and Romo tossed an interception on his next series. Romo was following the script authored by many rookies passers before him — his teams are blown out. The Cowboys trailed 14-0 at the end of the first quarter.

But the end of the first half Romo had settled in and he showed signs he was not an over-his-head rookie. He threw a touchdown pass to tight end Jason Witten, and the Cowboys trailed 14-10 at the half. Maybe Parcells was right about Romo.

The third quarter passed without a point, and then something clicked. Romo and the Cowboys blew up and they scored 25 fourth-quarter points. The Kid with the big smile was hitting passes, and led the Cowboys to an improbable 35-14 win. Romo finished 22-of-36 passing for 270 yards with a touchdown and an interception. Not bad for a first start.

On the sidelines, coach Bill Parcells looked like a man standing at the roulette wheel betting all of his chips and the deed to his house, hoping to hit 9 Blue. He had gambled that Romo could play, and for one game the marble fell on 9 Blue. Unlike the previous week when Parcells looked like he wanted to quit right there on the sidelines, he smiled, cajoled and even kissed a few of his players that evening in Charlotte.

"We haven't been having a lot of fun around here. They're having fun right now," Parcells said

(opposite) Parcells knew he was gambling by playing Romo, but once he finally made the decision he stuck by his young quarterback.

after the game. "That's the thing that I enjoy the most – when I see the faces of those players."

No one knew how The Great Romo Experiment of 2006 would turn out that night. It was only one game, but the Cowboys might have a legit quarterback. "You never know, the change that we made at quarterback," Romo said after the game. "You never know what you're going to get ... with a new starter who is untested. I was anxious just like Bill was to see what we were going to do out there tonight."

The Cowboys were 4-3, and all of the talk of doom around the three-game road trip returned to unbridled optimism. Maybe they'd go undefeated in this stretch?

The day after the game in Carolina the head coach immediately began the process that he would ultimately fail at: Beating back Romo Mania with cynicism, sarcasm and seasoned realism. It was his attempt to stay dry with an umbrella in a typhoon. He wanted to keep his quarterback on the ground. Every week for nearly a month, however, Romo's popularity and fame only increased no matter what Parcells said.

"There is some demonstrated ability (in Romo) that always fosters that kind of belief. But, you know, anyone can land a lucky punch," Parcells said. "Or every once in a while, you're standing up there at the plate and they hit your bat. You didn't really hit the ball. They hit your bat."

Parcells needed more than a lightning strike. If the Cowboys were going to be anything more

than a collection of overhyped players who compiled yet another .500 team, Romo had to be as good as he was in his starting debut again. And again. And again.

Week 9: At Washington, November 5, 2006

Redskins Hall of Fame coach Joe Gibbs made a strong bid to win the Mr. Obvious title when after this game he said, "Gosh, I don't know if I've experienced anything like that."

No one had. The Redskins' victory against the Cowboys was certainly not the work of Romo. He and the rest of his teammates had this game in the bag, and they should have been partying with a 5-3 record. Instead, Romo was on the field for one of the most bizarre conclusions to any game in recent memory that didn't include the Stanford band.

The Cowboys led 19-12 at the end of the third quarter. It should have been more. Terrell Owens dropped a pretty, sure-thing 74-yard touchdown in the third quarter to keep the Redskins in the game; it would have put the the Cowboys up by 14 points in the third quarter against a team that was eager to quit.

Of course, the Redskins tied the score, and they had a shot to take the lead with 35 seconds remaining. But kicker Nick Novak pushed a 49-yard field goal attempt wide right.

That put Romo in the position to show his fourth-quarter flair. It's the same flair that every great quarterback has – the ability to move his team within scoring range late in the game. On a 3rd-and-5 from his own 45-yard line, Romo threw a pass over the middle to Jason Witten for 28 yards. Romo had the Cowboys on the Redskins' 17-yard line with six seconds remaining. Romo would hold for Vanderjagt's 35-yard field goal attempt.

What happened next would become a part of every Sunday night highlight reel, and is sure to be immortalized on such DVDs as "Sports' Cruelest Conclusions."

Cowboys tackle Marc Colombo missed his assignment, and defensive back Troy Vincent ran through the line untouched to easily block the kick. In the ensuing scramble for the ball, Redskins safety Shaun Taylor picked it up and began his circuitous run the other way. Taylor was brought down at the Dallas' 44-yard line with no time remaining. But during his run, another lineman screwed up. Cowboys guard Kyle Kosier grabbed Taylor's face mask and drew a 15-yard personal foul penalty. A game can't end on a defensive penalty, and the Redskins were granted one single untimed down. Novak's 47-yard field goal attempt slipped over the crossbar for a 22-19 victory.

This loss was no fault of Romo's, but it was on his record. He finished 24-of-35 for 284 yards and two touchdowns. But the facts remained that the Cowboys were 4-4 at the midway point of the season. Their saving grace was the rest of the NFC

stunk just as much as they did, and they seemed to have a quarterback who could take advantage of it.

Week 10: At Arizona, November 12, 2006

There was no better antidote for the Cowboys and their fatalistic coach than the Arizona Cardinals. They were 1-7 when the Cowboys traveled to play the Cardinals in their their Cardinals' nice new diggs in Glendale.

By the time the Cowboys left Arizona they felt much better about themselves, and their quarterback. In a 27-10 win against the Cardinals, Romo showed his once-skeptical boss what he could do. "You couldn't have anticipated and wouldn't the kind of poise and execution and the way Tony plays within himself," Cowboys owner/general manager Jerry Jones said. "All of that was too much to expect."

The Cowboys were quickly becoming Romo's team. As Jones talked to reporters, Romo was putting on his sport coat and said, "C'mon. Let's go Jerry." A winning quarterback can get away with telling the boss when the team bus is leaving.

With every play Romo was taking away the "cautious" from "cautious optimism." The Cowboys hoped Romo could play well. But no one could say they saw this. Against the Cardinals, Romo passed for 308 with two touchdowns and no interceptions. For his performance he was named the NFC Offensive Player of the Week.

The Cowboys did what they were supposed to do – kick the hell out of a bad team. They had finished their three-game road swing 2-1. Not as good as it could have been, better than expected when a "rookie" quarterback took over three weeks prior. Romo had passed for more than 250 yards in three consecutive games to become the first Cowboys passer to do that since Troy Aikman in 1993.

Parcells was nervous about some things in Romo's game, namely, fighting the temptation to make every play a big play. When a player does that, turnovers loom. But overall, not even Coach Skeptical could complain too much. "I'm generally happy, you know that," Parcells said then. "You could not be generally happy." Parcells was still in the midst of evaluating a player that he felt was getting away with mistakes. And he felt that when he made a mistake, the pain would be spread equally among his teammates. When a fan or a member of the media saw a touchdown pass, Parcells had visions of Romo turnovers, or touchdowns for the wrong team.

The Cowboys were still 5-4, and a return date with .500 awaited them, according to conventional wisdom. The next game would be one of the biggest at Texas Stadium since the dynasty days of the mid 1990s.

Week 11: vs. Indianapolis, November 19, 2006

Not since the Cowboys' glory days of the 1990s had one game generated this much local and national interest. The Colts were 9-0, and featured some of the sexiest names in the NFL: Marvin Harrison, Reggie Wayne, Dallas Clark, Dwight Freeney, and quarterback Peyton Manning.

The Colts were the Colts primarily because they had The Man at quarterback in Manning. If the Cowboys had any chance to be the Cowboys of the glory days again, Romo would have to be their Manning. Beating the Colts would be a huge step.

By the time the game was over, Romo had not "out-dueled" Manning, but he did become the first quarterback in 2006 to beat him.

Manning was the same player Romo studied in his early days in the NFL. He watched tape after tape of Manning in the late-night video sessions with coach David Lee studying the way he moved, and functioned on the field. Unbeknownst to Manning, this was the Teacher vs. the Pupil.

On a gorgeous sunny afternoon at Texas Stadium, the Teacher was handling the Pupil in the first half. Romo lost a fumble and was intercepted in the game's first 30 minutes. Meanwhile, Manning eventually showed why he was Manning. He led an 88-yard touchdown drive at the end of the first half that ended with a 23-yard touchdown pass to receiver Reggie Wayne with 16 seconds remaining.

This may have been the Tony Romo Show, but Peyton Manning was still Peyton Manning. Manning was winning because he was better, as were his toys.

(opposite) Beating the Colts would be a huge step for Romo, but to do so he would have to conjure up his inner Peyton Manning.

But the Cowboys tied the game at seven on a defensive touchdown early in the third quarter when reserve linebacker Kevin Burnett intercepted a deflected pass and returned it 39 yards for a score. Then Manning went ahead late in the third quarter with a 4-yard touchdown pass to tight end Dallas Clark.

It was all set up for Romo, if he could show that fourth quarter flair. The Cowboys tied the game at 14 early in the fourth quarter after Romo led a 15-play drive. On the Cowboys' next possession, he led them on an eight-play drive that ended with Marion Barber's second rushing touchdown of the game to give the Cowboys a 21-14 lead. "What was so impressive to me was he had bad things – early fumble, interception – but he stayed within himself," Jerry Jones said after the game.

But it was two of Romo's plays that did not go for scores that finished off the Colts. They were the plays that a Manning did every single game.

The Cowboys had the ball at their own 8-yard line with 2:59 remaining, and the Colts had all three of their timeouts. On the second play of the drive, Romo completed a deep pass to rookie tight end Anthony Fasano for 22 yards. Two plays later, the Cowboys faced a third-and-seven from the Colts' 32-yard line and 2:09 remaining. If the Colts stopped Romo here, they would force a 49-yard field goal attempt. Romo changed the play from a run to a pass at the line of scrimmage. He wanted to

pass, and receiver Terry Glenn caught a 7-yarder from Romo for a first down.

Texas Stadium jumped and felt like the same building it did in the glory days of the 1990s. Tony Romo and the Dallas Cowboys had become the first NFL team to defeat Peyton Manning and the Indianapolis Colts. "It was magical," said Charlie Waters, the former Cowboys safety who played in the 1970s and handled the color duties on the radio broadcasts that year.

In the second half, Romo completed 10-of-11 passes for 130 yards.

Romo met Manning on the field after the game. "You're a good player," the Teacher told the Pupil.

Romo ran off the field holding a ball high over his head, and flashing a smile that Cowboys fans and the rest of the NFL would only see more of.

The Cowboys were two games over .500. Romo had defeated the Colts, and won his teammates. "He has the swagger," linebacker Brady James said of Romo. "He's been the coolest dude around for a while, people just haven't seen it. The way he's been playing is the way he's done it on the practice field for a long time."

But what Romo did next on the playing field no Cowboy had done in an even longer time.

Week 12: vs. Tampa Bay, November 23, 2006

The Thanksgiving Day game tradition at Texas Stadium has been going since 1966. The day

AP/Wide World

includes some of the franchise's most bizarre moments by some of the luminaries that adorn the Ring of Honor, names such as Staubach, Aikman, Meredith, Clint Longley, and others. The Ring serves as the team's Hall of Fame. And for a few moments before the game against the Buccaneers, the Ring of Honor included Romo, too. Some fans created a sign that hung outside of their suite that read "Tony Romo" and it appeared at first glance as if he was part of the Ring. The sign was taken down before kickoff. By the end of this game, however,

Jerry Jones had to be considering making Romo's name a permanent addition.

Playing against a bad Bucs team that was depleted by injury, Romo did something few quarterbacks ever do when he threw for five touchdowns.

The first was a 30-yarder to receiver Terry Glenn to tie the game at seven in the first quarter. The second was a 2-yard pass to Glenn. The third was a 1-yard pass to running back Marion Barber, and the Cowboys led 21-10 at the half.

(above) Romo impressed in the game against Indianapolis with a Manning-like second half, completing 10 of his 11 passes.

With 9:55 remaining in the third quarter, Romo completed TD pass No. 4 – a 2-yarder to Barber. Near the end of the quarter, touchdown pass No. 5 was a 7-yarder to Terrell Owens. Owens brought out his best holiday hyperbole after the 38-10 win when he said, "It was Romomentum."

Bucs coach Jon Gruden topped that when he said, "I thought it was Aikman out there." Aikman required an overtime for his five-touchdown performance, and Staubach never did it.

But there was Romo, proving that maybe he would forever walk in 15-minutes of fame. After this game Romo-Mania began to fly, much to the consternation of his head coach.

"Put the anointing oil away, OK?" Parcells begged.

Too late. "I can't wait to hear Bill talk about, 'Oh, how everybody is getting ahead of themselves having him in the Ring of Honor' and that type of thing," Jones said in the locker room. "I don't know if they are ahead of themselves."

People were proudly calling themselves "Romosexuals." Romo jerseys were popping up all over North Texas.

These were Romomentous times in Dallas. When Romo had a few friends visiting *Entourage*-style, he took them to a Dallas-area mall to do some shopping the weekend after the win against the Bucs. Word quickly spread the starting quarterback of the Dallas Cowboys was in the mall, and he and his friends had to be escorted past the crowds.

"It's just the way things are in Texas. But that's OK," Parcells said of Romo's popularity in November. "Just the way things are Philadelphia or in Boston or in New York – that's how it is in Texas. I'm not taking exception. It's OK. Someone has to be the voice of reason. When someone you think is real important says things about you, it fluffs you up and you think, 'Hey, I know.' It happens to all of us."

Everybody wanted a little piece of Romo. He became a favorite of ESPN and national magazines. He was named the NFC's Offensive Player of the Month. His popularity would only grow ... at least for another week.

Week 13: at New York Giants, December 3, 2006

In the cement bowels of Giants Stadium in East Rutherford, New Jersey, Romo headed to the field with that same smile on his face. Kickoff was a few hours away. But that smile was still there, because it always is. It's how his mouth is positioned. By the time this game ended, his smile was even wider.

Playing the feature game on Fox, the Cowboys were in the position to distance themselves from the New York Giants, and begin to make a push for one of the top two spots in the NFC. Romo had never played in a place like New York, either. It's a hard, cold place where the wind howls, and the fans crucify water boys if needed.

(opposite) Romo scrambles for extra yards during a tough win against the Giants in early December.

Even though this was one of Romo's worst statistical days, it would end as one of his best games to date. In the process of winning 23-20, Romo demonstrated that when the game evolved from the third to the fourth quarter, something in him changed, too. His "It" clicked.

He threw a first-quarter interception, but the Cowboys led 10-7 at the half, and 13-10 at the end of the third quarter. When he trotted on the field with 9:38 remaining in a tie game, he really hadn't been much of anything other than average; he was 14-of-26 for 166 yards, with a fumble and a pair of interceptions. But something changed. He led a 12-play, 66-yard drive in which he was 3-for-3 on third downs. The drive ended on Marion Barber's 7-yard touchdown run with 3:33 remaining.

Perhaps sensing their season was in jeopardy of evaporating, the Giants offense decided it cared. Quarterback Eli Manning and the Giants tied the game when he completed a 5-yard touchdown to receiver Plaxico Burress.

This was either going to be Romo Time, or more of Bledsoe Time.

Romo had the ball at his own 32-yard line with 66 seconds remaining. He bent over in the huddle.

"I need some time," Romo told center Andre Gurode. "I'm going to scramble for a second guys."

Then Romo looked at tight end Jason Witten. "I'm going to go to my left, and I'm going to throw it on the inside over your right shoulder."

Gurode looked at the rest of his offensive line, "We gotta' keep him clean, fellas."

On the first play from scrimmage, Romo was flushed from the pocket, ran to his left and, on the run, lofted a perfect deep pass to Witten for 42 yards. It was on the inside, over his right shoulder. Romo had put his team in position again to win.

With six seconds remaining, Martin Gramatica, who earlier in the week was signed to replace the released Mike Vanderjagt, ran on to the field to try a 46-yard field goal. The snap was fine, Romo's hold was clean, and Gramatica nailed the kick. The sideline responded accordingly, complete with a jubilant Parcells.

The Cowboys were 8-4, and Romo's numbers were ridiculous.

In six career starts, Romo was 129-of-187 passing (69.0%) for 1,651 yards, 10 touchdowns and four interceptions for a quarterback rating of 105.3. That's short for damn good. And in his first six NFL starts, he had a 5-1 record. That's short for amazing.

"This game showed me what he's about for years to come," receiver Terry Glenn said after the game. "Greatness."

Humility, however, was about to make a surprise visit. ■

(opposite) Romo was all smiles after piling up some impressive stats in his six career starts.

Out of the Blue

Romo turns few heads at the 2003 NFL combine

Long before he bobbled a ball in Seattle, Romo had already visited with humility starting with the NFL Combine, the biggest meat market in professional sports.

Hundreds of the best players from the college ranks, along with their agents, descend on downtown Indianapolis in the middle of February for five or six days. It used to be the Combine offered a good chance for nearly the entire NFL community to convene, talk to prospective draft picks on an individual level, and eat the corn-fed steak at St. Elmos and famous shrimp cocktail in downtown Indianapolis on the company tab.

By the time the NFL Combine kicked off its 2003 version it was well on its way to being the full-blown, over-hyped event that it is today. It is part beauty pageant, part job fair, and part football convetion complete with armies of predatory agents running around downtown Indianapolis. Hundreds of media scurry to the Indianapolis Convention Center to lounge around the hallway between the RCA Dome and the skywalk to the hotels in hopes of grabbing a team executive, a coach, a scout, anybody and anything in an effort to generate more NFL-related content. If the Combine were in Antarctica, the media would complete their own March of the Penguins in an effort for some food – in this case, a few nuggets of information on the Jets, Patriots, Cowboys, etc.

In February of 2003, however, the NFL Combine had also become an event where the biggest, baddest, meanest, and strongest could attent, and then promptly not work out. Long gone were the days when players came to Indy to run the 40-yard dash, bench press, throw and catch passes. But in the past seven to 10 years, it's become fashionable for the top players to travel to Indy to mostly see and be seen. Then they wait until their "Pro Day" at their respective college campus to run the 40-yard dash, lift weights, and throw the ball to "their" receivers.

(opposite) Parcells would make Romo earn his chance to run the team, and the young quarterback would not disappoint.

When Tony Romo arrived at the 2003 Combine, he had no such luxuries. The quarterbacks people wanted to see were USC's Carson Palmer, Marshall's Byron Leftwich, Cal's Kyle Boller, and Florida's Rex Grossman. Romo had been invited to show what he could do, but he was also there to be the "bullpen pitcher."

"He threw to the linebackers. To the tight ends. To the running backs. He threw to everybody," said Gil Brandt, who helps run the combine. Three lesser-known quarterbacks are usually invited for this job. It's a beating. You throw all day, for four or five days. Cowboys scout Jim Hess was on the RCA Dome field one of those sessions.

"Man, you're arm is going to fall off," Hess told Romo.

"I'm fine. This isn't going to bother me," Romo said.

Hess said the two other quarterbacks who were "the bullpen" throwers left before the end of the Combine. "Tony stayed the entire time," Hess said. "I liked him. A lot. He was a good kid. But I don't even think I wrote up a report on him."

Brandt did. He wrote: "Looks good moving around and throwing the ball. Great job with the media." When Brandt brought Romo down to the interview room he sat him at one of the circular tables. In that room are podiums at each end; the "in demand" players such as Palmer or Leftwich go there. Everybody else goes to a table. What struck Brandt was how Romo sat at a table, and answered questions for what he estimates to be 2 1/2 hours.

"Now, they don't just ask just anybody to go to the combine and throw passes to all the players," Brandt said. "They're not going to pick some bozo and put him out there. He has to have some ability. He has to have a chance. After watching him a little bit there, I thought he would get picked in the sixth or seventh round of the draft that year. I thought someone might take a chance on him."

Playing at Eastern Illinois worked against Romo. Scouts and professional coaches are instantly wary of players who don't consistently play against the big-time competition that the quarterbacks at Michigan, USC, or Florida State face every Saturday. The Eastern Illinois Panthers played in the Ohio Valley Conference. The home of the Too Short, the Not Big Enough, and the Not Fast Enough. To be considered draft pick–worthy from I-AA football, Romo was going to have to grade as an exceptional athlete. He didn't. His time in the 40-yard dash was 5.0 seconds (slow by NFL standards), and he posted unimpressive 30-inch vertical jump.

At the end of the combine, Romo was written up by the scouting services who rate players and draw up mock draft boards. On some of the mock boards, Romo went undrafted and was labeled a "priority free agent." Some scouting services projected him as a potential fourth-round pick. That

(opposite) *The NFL combine is part beauty pageant, part job fair, and part football convention.*

was a long shot; he was more apt to go in the sixth or seventh round. The Cowboys had him labeled as a fifth round player, but it was doubtful they would pick him.

Usually by the time the sixth or seventh round rolls around, teams are trying to find athletes. This is when the lifetime college basketball player is picked with the intent of moving him to tight end. "What happens in those rounds is that you get a lot of guys who look a lot alike," Brandt said. "Now, if there was a way to measure a guy's heart, a guy who would work the hardest and really compete you wouldn't have a guy who was an undrafted free agent."

That is exactly what happened to Romo. In all 13 quarterbacks were selected in the 2003 draft. They were, in order:

1. **Carson Palmer, USC, Cincinnati Bengals**
7. **Byron Leftwich, Marshall, Jacksonville Jaguars**
19. **Kyle Boller, Cal, Baltimore Ravens**
22. **Rex Grossman, Florida, Chicago Bears**
88. **Dave Raggone, Louisville, Houston Texans**
97. **Chris Simms, Texas, Tampa Bay Buccaneers**
110. **Seneca Wallace, Iowa State, Seattle Seahawks**
163. **Brian St. Pierre, Boston College, Pittsburgh Steelers**
192. **Drew Henson, Michigan, Houston Texans**
200. **Brooks Bollinger, Wisconsin, New York Jets**
201. **Kliff Kingsbury, Texas Tech, New England Patriots**
232. **Gibran Hamdan, Indiana, Washington Redskins**
241. **Ken Dorsey, Miami, San Francisco 49ers**

On the first day of the 2003 NFL draft, Romo had no chance of being picked by the Cowboys or any other team. But Hess and first-year offensive assistant coach Sean Payton both liked Romo, and continually kept in contact with him as the draft progressed. They wanted to keep him informed as to why they were doing what they were doing. Payton had a special interest in Romo. He, too, was a record-setting quarterback at Eastern Illinois back in the mid-'80s and identified with the "small college" label that was firmly attached to Romo's resume. The Cowboys wanted to draft Romo. His draft card written by the Cowboys had the buzz words teams looked for – fire, competetiveness, smarts, heady, heart. What it didn't say was what a lot of teams seemed to be thinking: "Small school guy. Doesn't have a chance. Career backup."

But Bill Parcells was only a few months into the job of rebuilding a franchise and a roster that had finished 5-11 in three consecutive seasons. There was a lot of garbage on that team. Plus, they had Quincy Carter on the roster as well as Chad Hutchinson. Carter had two years of starting experience, and was a former second round draft pick. Hutchinson was a former Stanford quarterback, who left to pursue a pitching career in the St. Louis Cardinals organization. Hutchinson had played nine games the season before Parcells arrived.

Owner Jerry Jones told Bill Parcells he didn't know what he had in either player. And that could he look

(opposite) Romo was anything but a big deal at the NFL Combine, posting average numbers during the physical testing.

at both? To Parcells, the request was not only reasonable, but logical. The Cowboys had needs everywhere. They needed to stockpile good bodies, so they passed on Romo. "When Bill got there, we were very much into the business of misevaluating quarterbacks," former Cowboys scout Brian Broaadus said. "It's always the most mis-evaluated position in the draft. Look at Romo's class – how many of those guys turned out they could play?"

(Palmer has developed into one of the best passers in the NFL for the Bengals. Leftwich was unable to stay healhy for the Jaguars, and was released before the start of the 2007 season. The Ravens tried with Boller, but signed veteran Steve McNair before the start of the 2006 season to replace him. Despite erratic play, Grossman led the Bears to the Super Bowl in the 2006 season, but was benched in the first month of the 2007 season. Simms was starting for the Bucs before he ruptured his spleen in a game in September of 2006; he hasn't played since. Wallace has been moved back and forth from quarterback to wide receiver in Seattle. Drew Henson ... keep reading.)

Romo knew what he was up against. "I could be a boom or a bust," he told the *Milwaukee Journal Sentinel.* "It's tough to take a chance on someone like that."

About 20 teams showed interest in Romo as a rookie free agent. But two franchises were the most fervent in their pursuit of the former Eastern Illiniois star – Dallas and Denver. He had talked with Broncos coach Mike Shanahan at length about coming to Denver. Shanahan had a thing for quarterbacks from Eastern Illinois. He played for the Panthers in the 1970s. "I'll be honest with you – I tried to sign him very hard," Shanahan said. "I really liked him coming out of school. In fact, we offered him $20,000."

That's a fortune for a rookie free agents. Teams such as the Jets offer $2,000 to all rookie free agents. There is no negotiating.

But the Cowboys had put in their time with Romo. Romo was intrigued about the possibility of playing under Parcells, who along with Jones made "recruiting calls" to Romo. So on May 1, Romo signed contract that included a signing bonus worth between $10,000 to $12,000 bonus. The contract also covered his room and board, a per diem. Overall, it's a contract that's worth between $3,500 and $4,500 through the end of training camp. If he made it that far. If he did, then he'd go up to the hundreds of thousands of dollars.

The process of actually making the team began one week later when when the Cowboys had their first rookie minicamp under Parcells. Not many people noticed Romo in those early days. They noticed that the team's top rookie draft pick, defensive back Terence Newman, had to fetch the head coach water during breaks. Or that the rookies didn't have the star on their helmets. They had

(opposite) The Denver Broncos' Mike Shanahan, who knew of Romo through his own Eastern Illinois connection, was among the few who had their eye on the unsung quarterback when he came out of college.

to earn those. These were Parcells staples; cute little old school tricks the media adored.

Both Sean Payton and offensive assistant David Lee noticed Romo. They liked the speed of his release and his footwork. On the last day of the rookie minicamp, Lee approached Parcells on the practice field and told him, "This Romo has something in the pocket. He has something back there you can't coach."

"Lee, I need to take you to a real game." Parcells said. "The way he's throwing now, he'll get six balls batted down every 10 throws.

"That was the last time I approached Parcells with something like that," Lee said.

That would be the last time Lee offered his opinion to Parcells when it wasn't requested, but not the first time he found himself impressed by this unheralded kid.

On that final day of that initial minicamp, Romo walked off the field with Lee. Then he started to press. "How'd I do? What do you think? What did Sean Payton say?" Lee told Romo he had done well. That they liked what they saw.

"What did Parcells say?" Romo asked.

"I can't tell you that," Lee said.

"What did Parcell say?" Romo pushed.

"Tony, you did fine," Lee answered.

"C'mon. What did Parcells say?" Romo said.

This continued until Lee finally relented about Romo's mechanics.

"The first thing Romo said was, 'OK, can you fix it?'" Lee said.

Lee had worked with quarterbacks on their mechanics before. He knew the risks involved. You don't just change mechanics in one single practice, or a month's worth of practices.

"This is going to take a year," Lee said. The mechanics that made Romo a successful college passer were going to have to be changed, and that might not work. "You're talking about changing the way a guy has thrown for however long," Lee said. "That's muscle memory. You can't change that. It takes about 10,000 throws. Maybe a year to do it."

Lee told Romo if he made the team coming out of training camp in San Antonio he would break down and rebuild Romo's mechanics. To change Romo's mechanics any time before then and the results could be disastrous. Passes could sail right, left, but mostly high if Romo's mechanics were off and that might hurt his chances of making the team.

"Let's do it now," Romo told Lee.

Lee relented not so much because he thought it was a good idea but because he wanted to help an eager student.

Over the next two to three months he worked with Lee on slotting his arm a little higher, on releasing the football a little differently. Lee had devised his own system of working on a release that involved a net; it's designed to keep the passing elbow up. Romo needed to throw the ball in more

(opposite) Another coach with ties back to Eastern Illinois, Sean Payton was quick to recognize Romo's potentially huge upside when Payton was still an assistant coach with the Cowboys.

Although they didn't have a star at the position, the Cowboys felt safe in having several options at quarterback.

of an over-the-top fashion. He needed to raise it a good 12 inches, at least.

Before practice, with as Parcells, Payton and others sometimes watching, Lee would stand under the goal post and Romo would stand in front of Lee's "net" and throw passes.

Romo threw, and Lee caught the ball ... over his head. "Incomplete! Too high Tony!" Lee screamed.

Romo threw, and Lee caught the ball ... over his head. "Incomplete!"

Romo threw, and Lee caught the ball ... in front of his face. "Complete! You are pulling the ball down."

Romo threw, and Lee caught the ball ... over his head. "Incomplete. Hold onto the ball for a half an inch longer in your hand and in your mind!"

This went on, and on and on. By the time When Romo headed to San Antonio for the Cowboys training camp in 2003, he hadn't done this enough to the point where it was routine. "I was holding my breath down there for him," Lee said. "Everything he threw was high." It took nearly two years worth of drills between Romo and Lee before his mechanics were rebuilt.

Parcells had a vision for Romo, though, even then, even with his troublesome mechanics. He saw at least enough ability, persistence and confidence to keep him on the roster as a rookie.

"He kind of lives, breathes football. He's got a quick release. You saw that early on when he first got there," Sean Payton said. "But there were some things he had to work on, some of his decisions. He tended to force some balls. I think the very first snap he had from the line of scrimmage in a preseason game, he fumbled the center-QB exchange, picked it up, scrambled, then threw an interception. So he had two turnovers on one play. His very first play ever in the NFL. So needless to say, he's come a long way."

Payton was wrong, and, right. By the time Romo played in an actual game he had come a long way. Romo's first play was a little better than Payton remembers.

His first NFL appearance in a game came with 11:34 remaining in the fourth quarter of a preseason game between the Cowboys and Cardinals in Phoenix on August 9, 2003. His first play was a 12-yard pass to rookie tight end Jason Witten. Two plays later, Romo was sacked on a drive that ended in a punt. He had one more series, but that ended with an interception. Romo's first NFL stat line read: 4-of-8 passing, 51 yards, one interception and one sack.

His second preseason game was a little smoother. He threw a 60-yard touchdown pass to Randall Williams. And by the end of his first NFL preseason, Romo was 9-of-17 for 134 yards, was sacked three times, intercepted once and threw for one touchdown. He wouldn't play another down in 2003. Romo spent the entire season as the club's third quarterback. He was sitting behind two players that the Cowboys had either, A. Invested a high draft pick to obtain or lots of game time to train; or B. Invested a lot of money in. The first was Quincy Carter. The other was Chad Hutchinson.

Carter was preparing to enter his third season as the Cowboys "kind of" quarterback. By that point, he had managed to flash potential, and drive his coaches crazy ... sometimes on the same play. He was the ultimate coach killer. He had enough ability for a coach or team to stay with him, but they would never win big with Carter. He was also immature, paranoid, thin skinned and you understand how fragile his "starting" position was. Carter was the quarterback for the Cowboys for the season-opener in 2002 when he lost to the expansion Houston Texans in their first-ever regular season game. By the end of the seventh game that season, he had lost his job to Hutchinson as well.

Hutchinson was a former big-time player at Stanford before electing to play pro baseball in the St. Louis Cardinals organization. When that flopped, he returned to football. Parcells saw Hutchinson as a guy who could play when everything went according to plan.

These two are called obligations. The Cowboys had been at the blackjack table for so long and saw so many of their chips next to the dealer that they kept reaching into their wallet in effort to get some of their money back. Parcells had to try. Carter would be the quarterback. And in one of the greatest coach-

ing achievements ever with the Cowboys, the team finished 10-6 that season and made the playoffs.

In the meantime, Romo spent his time working with David Lee and running the scout team offense. He'd throw a ball in practice, "and Bill would absolutely undress him," Lee said. "The next pass would be a 25-yard strike down the field."

Romo would make it a habit to drive back to the Cowboys' practice facility to meet with Lee to watch tapes, but not of himself. Lee found tapes of the most fundamentally sound quarterback he could – the Colts' Peyton Manning. Romo was around Lee so much that first year that Parcells would chide Lee, "You and Romo – you guys are tied at the hip."

After his first year of watching, one road block to Romo's ascension was subtracted when the team cut Hutchinson. But as quickly as one piece was moved from out in front of Romo, more were added.

The biggest obstacle he would face for the next two seasons came in April of 2004 when the Cowboys made a trade with the Texans for the rights to Drew Henson. Houston had selected the former Michigan star in the sixth round of the same draft Romo went un-chosen in 2003. It was a flyer pick by Houston; at the time of the selection, Henson had been playing third base in the New York Yankees' minor league system. When the Texans drafted him, he said he had no intention of leaving of leaving baseball. But things changed

when he realized he couldn't hit a curveball.

Henson wanted to play football, and the Cowboys were still searching for The Franchise at quarterback. So Jones traded a third round pick in the 2005 draft to acquire Henson. Not too long after Henson became a Cowboy so too did a Parcells' favorite, veteran passer Vinny Testaverde.

That ran the total to four quarterbacks on the Cowboys' 2004 offseason roster – Carter, Testaverde, Henson and Romo. There was no way the Cowboys would keep four quarterbacks. And there was no way Romo would clear waivers and be added to the team's practice squad. As it stood, Romo looked to be the most easily squeezed and therefore released by the Cowboys at the end of training camp. The only thing that might save him was if one of the three in front of him suffered an injury.

What happened next was far more unpredictable than a sprained ankle or sore shoulder happened.

One week into Cowboys' training camp in Oxnard, California, the team cut Carter. They stated they didn't like the way he was playing, or the way he handled the signing of Testaverde. And, oh yeah, he also failed a drug test, too. Carter actually checked into a hotel in the area, mostly in disbelief. He later said he would never speak to Parcells or Jerry Jones after the morning he was told he was cut. And years later, when he was the quarterback of the ArenaFootball2's Bossier-Shreveport team, he would admit to kicking himself every day for mak-

ing the mistakes he made. He should have been the quarterback of the Dallas Cowboys. He never quite realized at the time how big it was to be the quarterback of the Dallas Cowboys. Carter cut a sad picture – was he a star quarterback? No. Could he play in the NFL for 10 years and earn a six-figure check? Yes. But this was the first part of the process of blowing that opportunity.

But his screw-up ensured a spot on the Cowboys' roster for Romo. Testaverde would start. Henson would back him up. Romo would again be No. 3.

What people didn't know is that almost immediately Parcells balked at automatically buying into Henson the way fans and the media did. Henson was Big Time. The son of a coach, he played at Michigan, and had all of the measurables Romo didn't. Henson was 6-foot-4, 235 pounds. NFL scouts said had Henson not played baseball he would have been one of the top quarterbacks when he entered the draft.

Romo had none of this. Not that Romo had done much to advance his hopes for advancement up the ladder in the preseason. In his first preseason game, at Houston on August 8, 2004, he was awful. He threw two interceptions, and was sacked twice, including once for a safety. Romo met with his parents outside Reliant Stadium after the game.

"How did I do?" Tony asked his father.

"You sucked," Ramiro said. "Are they going to give you a ride back? If not, I have room in the car."

(opposite) One of the elder statesman of the NFL, Vinny Testaverde would take snaps ahead of Romo when Drew Henson failed to pan out.

Romo needed to show something, or risk the Cowboys signing a more established third quarterback. In the Cowboys' second preseason game, at Oakland, he took over at his own 41-yard line with the Cowboys trailing 20-15 and 4:01 remaining. This drive nearly ended his career twice, but ultimately it saved it. He threw an interception, but the play was nullified thanks to a defensive holding call. With 23 seconds remaining, he completed a 13-yard pass to tight end Sean Ryan to the 1-yard line. The Cowboys were out of timeouts.

"Kill the clock. Spike the ball," his coaches told him through the headsets.

Instead, he went to the line, called his own play. This was playground elements his teammates would eventually love. Romo scored a touchdown on a quarterback keeper with seven seconds remaining. The play was challenged by instant replay, but the touchdown was upheld. Romo had won the game with a last-minute drive. "If he had not scored and we hadn't stopped the clock and lost on the 1-yard line, he might have been cut that night. But he scored," Lee said. Funny to think how a little thing like the meaningless conclusion to an equally meaningless preseason game turned out in retrospect to be a decisive moment for the future of a man and an entire franchise.

Romo had shown his head coach something, too. As bad as he was in Houston, he learned from and improved on his mistakes. He finished his second preseason 24-of-39 passing for 250 yards, was sacked three times and threw one touchdown and two interceptions.

"Early on, you saw a live arm, a guy with quick decisions," Payton said. "You know, he can make some funny body throws when things aren't perfect around him. You know, these guys play in a pocket that's ever-changing. So when you find a guy that can move a little and throw it, step up a little and make a play, that's the reality of the game that we see day in and day out."

No one was expecting either Romo or Henson to play that season. Henson hadn't played football in four years. Romo would technically be the No. 2 on the depth chart for the first six games of the season. He even found a way onto the field, just not as a quarterback. In the Cowboys season-opener at Minnesota, they used punter Mat McBriar as the holder on field goals and extra points. McBriar bobbled and lost a snap on a field goal try in the first quarter, and Romo took over those duties full time in the second quarter.

But after seven games into the season, Romo's job as the No. 2 was gone. Henson had taken the spot. Something about Romo's game irked Parcells.

"He has an ability to move the ball with the strength of his arm," former Cowboys receiver Keyshawn Johnson said. "I was skeptical of him because of his flash and dash. He'd want to force the ball into tight situations. And that means you can be

(opposite) Romo was anything but good in his first preseason action, but he would continue to work hard in practice.

AP/Wide World

prone to turnovers. So on him I was a yes, but no. I thought he could play if somebody doesn't care about his gunslinger mentality. I don't think Bill cared much then because he wasn't the starter."

It was the gunslinger part – the perceived carelessness with the ball – that bothered Parcells.

By the time the Cowboys played the Ravens in Baltimore on Nov. 21, the season was just about gone. The Cowboys were 3-6, and Henson was viewed as the future. And when the Cowboys fell behind 30-3 midway in the fourth quarter, the game was over for all intents and purposes. Testaverde was hurt, but not badly. It was the perfect time to play Henson. The rookie was 6-for-6 with 47 yards passing and one touchdown in garbage time. It may have been garbage time, but it was enough for fans to scream for Henson to start playing so as to begin the maturation process of their next franchise quarterback. The owner wanted it, too.

Parcells would start the rookie in the annual Thanksgiving Day game, but some people in and around the Cowboys feared it was more in an attempt to demonstrate that Henson couldn't play more than an attempt to develop a passer. Henson was overmatched; with his team ahead 7-0 near the end of the first half, he threw a pass to the right side of the flat that was intercepted by Bears defensive back R.W. McQuarters and returned 45 yards for the touchdown. And these Bears were not the Super Bowl Bears, either. They were in the midst of going

5-11 that season under first-year coach Lovie Smith.

Parcells had seen enough to confirm what he had suspected. Henson was 4-of-12 passing for 31 yards, was sacked once, and had a quarterback rating of 7.6. What Parcells saw in Chad Hutchinson he saw in Henson – player with great ability who could cut apart teams in 7-on-7 passing drills but who struggled to function once the boat hit the beach.

Parcells started Testaverde to begin the second half, much to the iritation of Jerry Jones. He knew the season was not going to end with a playoff berth, so he wanted the same thing the fans wanted – play the rookie quarterback and take your beatings now. Parcells wanted to win that game in the hopes that maybe the Cowboys could generate some momentum and make a run to the playoffs.

It was Henson's second and last regular season appearance with the Cowboys. On Dec. 19, Romo was promoted to the No. 2 spot for the December games against the Eagles and against the Redskins. For the season finale, he was back to No. 3. His biggest progress that season had been having his locker next to Testaverde all season. Both Parcells and Romo later credited that year of sitting next to the veteran for teaching him how to study, prepare, and play – in effect, becoming franchise quarterback material.

The Cowboys finished 6-10 in 2004. Testaverde was not brought back. Parcells didn't want Henson,

(opposite) Some teammates worried that Romo was more style than substance when he had trouble holding onto the football in his early appearances.

but another name would soon come available: Drew Bledsoe.

Parcells had drafted Bledsoe at New England with the first pick in the 1993 draft. Three years later, they went to the Super Bowl together. Parcells didn't fly back with the Patriots, and was gone from the franchise. Bledsoe stayed, and in 2001 he suffered an early-season injury that opened the door for former sixth-round pick Tom Brady. The Patriots and coach Bill Belichick thought so little of Bledsoe they traded him to a division rival, the Buffalo Bills, for the 2002 season. After three years of no playoffs in Buffalo, the Bills released him.

It was logical for the Cowboys to be interested in Bledsoe. Not only did he still have a live arm, but the Cowboys knew they weren't going to win with Testaverde. Parcells didn't feel like Henson or Romo were ready. He knew Bledsoe, and he was the veteran quarterback he preferred. So the Cowboys signed him to a three-year contract to be their starter in 2005.

There would be no competition for the starter's job. Any quarterback controversy focused on the right to be called Bledsoe's backup. "What is it with this Henson-Romo talk? They haven't done anything yet," Parcells asked on August 7 that year. At that time, though, Henson was playing well. Well enough that Parcells repeatedly said he wanted to play either Henson or Romo in an actual game in the 2005 season. Who played first would signal

who was No. 2.

By this time in his third preseason, Romo's time practicing and watching film with David Lee had paid off. So, too, had spending time next to Testaverde. If Romo was going to make a jump, it had to be this training camp. Parcells came from the school of Tom Landry on players: If a player is going to make it in the NFL, he must begin to show something by his third season. Romo knew it, too.

"You only get such a grace period in the NFL before you've got to produce," Romo said in the early weeks of training camp in 2005.

If neither he nor Henson showed they could play, there was a thought that the Cowboys would re-sign Testaverde. That would mean Romo would be cut; there was no chance the Cowboys would release Henson ahead of Romo at that point. They had invested millions in Henson, and hundreds of thousands in Romo.

Approximately three weeks into his third minicamp, Romo had emerged as something more than the No. 3 quarterback. Against the Texans in Week 3 of the 2005 preseason, only he and Bledsoe played. Romo was 5-of-8 passing that game with a touchdown. He had moved past Henson. He looked to be flirting with the idea of passing Bledsoe.

But Romo wouldn't play a meaningful down of football in 2005. He was the holder for every field goal, and point after attempt. For the first time in his professional career, however, there were whis-

(opposite) After Henson proved that he was not an option at quarterback for the Cowboys, Romo was promoted to No. 2 on the depth chart.

pers as the Cowboys limped to a 9-7 no-playoff fin- ish that it was time to see Romo do something other than hold on a field goal try. Players started notic- ing Romo as well.

Long before he was benched, Bledsoe was in the process of losing the team. In one of those miser- able-wet December days at Giants Stadium in New Jersey, Bledsoe didn't make the types of plays his team needed, and the Cowboys lost a crucial game, 17-10. It was at that point his teammates began to question him.

"I'd say we were split about Drew," defensive end Chris Canty said. The Cowboys had a shot at the playoffs until about 30 minutes before kickoff of their final game of the year.

Then "it" started in February. That's when peo- ple began to hear that Parcells knew Bledsoe's best days were probably left on the fields in New England, when they were both younger. Bledsoe was going to be 35, and by then whatever it was about Bledsoe's game that had begun to crumble wasn't going to rally back. And yet any impending "quarterback controversy" was firmly filed in the "For a Later Day" drawer. They had other, and bet- ter distractions to occupy their time and anxieties of their loyal fans.

In March, the Cowboys signed Mr. Controversy, wide receiver Terrell Owens. His impending rela- tionship/disaster with Parcells dwarfed every single other story on the Dallas Cowboys in the offseason

of 2006. This was a player who devoured quarter- backs. But Bledsoe eagerly accepted Owens, saying he went into it with his eyes wide open. What his eyes weren't as open to immediately was that his job was up for grabs.

It wasn't until the first week of training camp in Oxnard, California, that it became apparent Romo was going to get his chance.

Sports Illustrated's football writer Peter King, who covered Parcells and the New York Giants in the 1980s, reported out of Cowboys camp that Parcells liked Romo. Possibly enough to make him his starter. Parcells was often cryptic to the local media, but to those who knew him from his Super Bowl winning days with the Giants where he was still revered, he was more trusting and open. When Peter King said Parcells liked Romo, there was something to it.

Parcells made it no secret that he wanted to get Romo ready to play, and that he intended to play him. A lot.

"I thought he had a high degree of intelligence, was a willing worker," Parcells recalled of that train- ing camp. "He had athletic ability and my other vision for him centered around other intangibles. Once you say that to yourself then it's, 'OK, this is worth making an attempt to do something with. Let's make a try at it with this guy.'"

But when Romo played the entire preseason opener against the Seahawks in Seattle that August,

(opposite) While more media attention was focused on the considerable egos of Owens and Parcells and their efforts to peacefully coexist, Romo was quietly emerging as the starting quarterback in Big D.

something smelled fishy and it wasn't Pike's Market. Romo completed 19-of-25 passes against the Seahawks for 235 yards and one touchdown. Those were a starter's numbers, and Parcells was asked if he had a QB decision to make.

"Here is my honest feeling: I learned something about Romo the other night. Here is what I learned; you have to coach him all the way through the game," Parcells said. "That means you can't take for granted just because things are going well they are going to continue to go well. You have to coach him all the way through the game. You have to keep him right on it, keep him focused on it, keep reminding him of things. He's a very bright kid and his mind races. And he'll have some ideas."

Off in the distance, the dreaded and cliched quarterback controversy approached. Romo knew he was going to get his chance. That Bledsoe was going to create a window. That Parcells wanted to see him play.

Before the final preseason game of 2006, Romo signed a two-year extension with the Cowboys that would keep him with the team through the end of 2007. He wanted the deal to be longer, but he wanted to know that if Bledsoe was still The Man he would have the chance to go somewhere else.

"I'm telling you, we're going to win here," Romo said after the preseason finale.

A few days before the start of the season, Parcells began to quickly dismiss any talk of a quarterback controversy. Bledsoe would start against the Jaguars in Jacksonville on opening day. Everyone on the staff agreed – Bledsoe, after all, was a veteran, and he had been signed by the Cowboys to be their starter. Parcells, though, thought he had something more than just an option in Romo just in case.

"That training camp and that preseason is when I became convinced I may have something here," Parcells said.

But Bledsoe began to sense his environment. Something like this had happened to him before, in 2000, in New England. He had suffered an early season injury and little-known Tom Brady replaced him as the quarterback. For good.

Unlike Bledsoe's first season with the Cowboys, he had little room to screw up. And when the Cowboys lost against the Jaguars 24-17, the demand for Romo only grew louder. Against the Jaguars, Bledsoe was 16-of-33 for 246 yards with three interceptions, and was sacked twice.

A man in Dallas produced cheap white T-shirts with a screen print of the Dallas skyline. One version of the shirt read Team Bledsoe. The other read Team Romo.

The day after the loss against the Jaguars, Bledsoe came to his locker to address reporters. That had never happened before since Bledsoe always talked on Wednesdays to reporters. But he was keenly aware of the temperature of the team, and his surroundings.

(opposite) Romo would play the entirety of the 2006 preseason opener and very quickly the winds of change would start blowing through Dallas.

For a while, he kept Romo-mania at bay. The Cowboys improved to 2-1, then dropped to 2-2 after a loss to the Eagles in Philadelphia. In that game, Bledsoe completed less than 50 percent of his passes, was sacked seven times, and threw three interceptions. Mr. Controversy wasn't helping. "Who's pulling the trigger?" Owens asked after the loss in Philadelphia. It was around that time former NFL players turned TV analysts Michael Irvin and Deion Sanders began to lobby for Romo; both Irvin and Sanders are friends with Owens.

At one point in that first month of the season, Ramiro Romo came to Dallas to visit his son and watch a practice. The team was stretching during warmups, and Parcells approached Tony's father.

"Mr. Romo, Tony is doing well, and I think he's improved to the point where I'm getting ready to put him in there," Parcells told Ramiro.

"You'll know when it's time coach," Ramiro said.

Translation: It's your team. You're the head coach. Ramiro was not going to pump his son up full of hyperbole or hot air that he should be starting, or the coach was giving his son a raw deal. Even in the professional ranks where athletes earn a minimum six-figure income, they are susceptible to the same type of angry, paranoid talk from friends and family how they are the greatest thing in the world, that they should be starting, that they are getting screwed, blah-blah-blah.

But back in the Cowboys' offices, there was no concern about Romo. What there were serious worries about was that maybe Bledsoe was always going to be one week up, one week down kind of player and they would never separate themselves from the rest of their division.

"I don't know if Bledsoe lost the team, but we needed someone to get us to from winning one week to losing the next week," center Andre Gurode said. "As a team we needed that to get better consistently. Not win one, lose one." One week later, the Cowboys cut up the Texans 34-6 with Bledsoe having his way against an overmatched defense. In that game, Romo made his first regular season appearance as something more than a holder. He completed both of his passes, including a 2-yard touchdown pass to Terrell Owens in garbage time.

The Cowboys were 3-2.

And the New York Giants were coming to town for a Monday Night game. ■

(oppsoite) Bledsoe's best days were behind him and soon he could only watch as Romo ascended into the role of starting quarterback.

Romo watching the Cowboys play the
Saints on December 10, 2006.

The Fall

After such a meteoric rise, a letdown may have been inevitable

Just as those who watched his debut against the New York Giants and could never have predicted Romo would ascend to the such a high level of productivity and fame so quickly, few could have guessed he would drop with such equal drama. The beginning was on NBC's Sunday Night Football; the "ending" would occur on the Peacock's national stage, too, complete with Al Michaels calling play by play, and John Madden providing color.

Still basking in their road win against the Giants, Romomania had swept North Texans, Cowboys fans, the local media etc. The last time the NFL was blindsided by an out-of-nowhere quarterback like Romo it was Kurt Warner with the Rams. "I think Kurt Warner is one of the neatest stories ever," Romo said.

There was the smile again from the small-town kid who had "dun' good." The league couldn't say enough good things about the equally "neat" Tony Romo. It had been six games, and even ESPN analyst Joe Theismann said he had seen enough. That endorsement didn't matter as much as it did from owner Jerry Jones. When Jones and the Cowboys unveiled the grand plans for his new, $1 billion stadium in Arlington, Texas, in early December, Jones said that he had seen enough from his quarterback to know that he could call off the search. He had found his quarterback for this season, and to lead his team into his new ode to excess.

Jones had spent so many millions on ex-baseball players, aging vets, and never-would-bes to find his quarterback that he'd throw whatever amount down to finally find his next Aikman when it came time to do a contract.

Romo was in the process of getting out of Aikman's shadow and creating his own. What Jones didn't know that in a few days the shadow that Romo began creating was doubt.

Week 14: vs. Saints, December 10, 2006

Cowboys' running back Julius Jones broke

(opposite) The NFL had been blindsided by Romo's success, but there would still be growing pains.

through the left side of the line of scrimmage and ran away from the entire defense for a 77-yard touchdown run and a 7-0 lead on their third offensive play. That would be the Cowboys' lone highlight of the entire night for Romo or anyone else against the Saints.

The second quarter was a blur of Saints points, and Cowboys ineptitude; the Saints scored 21 points, including a pair of touchdown catches from somebody named Mike Karney. The Saints recovered an onside kick, and scored 21 more points in the third quarter. Karney added one more receiving touchdown on the night as the Saints embarrassed the Cowboys, 42-17. It wasn't as close as the final score indicated.

Saints quarterback Drew Brees became the first Cowboys opponent to throw five touchdowns in a game. Karney's touchdowns were the first, second and third of his three year career.

"That was a pretty good whippin'," Bill Parcells said in an understatement after the game.

There were two major developments from that game – the was the first time that Romo had been off the entire night, and there would be no cute comeback story. There was nothing cute about this Sunday night. Romo completed fewer than 50 percent of his passes, and was picked off twice. His one touchdown should have been an interception; Saints defensive back Fred Thomas was wearing a cast on his arm and instead of catching a Romo pass, it deflected off his hands into the arms of Terrell Owens for a 34-yard touchdown.

Saints coach Sean Payton and his defensive coordinator, Gary Gibbs, had done the rest of the league a favor. Not only did they beat the Cowboys, they showed the NFL how to score on them, and how to keep Romo from scoring. If there were two men in the NFL who had an idea how to do both, it would have been Payton and Gibbs.

Payton spent the previous three years under Parcells on his offensive staff. He was the one who worked a considerable amount with Romo, and helped convince him to sign as a rookie with the Cowboys after the draft. Like Romo, Payton attended Eastern Illinois University. Shortly after Payton took the Saints head coaching job after the 2005 season, he called Parcells to inquire about possibly trading for Romo. In not so many words, Parcells told Payton to get some more sleep. Parcells wasn't trading his then No. 2 quarterback.

Like Payton, Gibbs had been on the Cowboys' staff for the previous three seasons as well. Both coaches knew the Cowboys' personnel better than any coach on any staff in the league.

"They took advantage of everything," Cowboys owner/general manager Jerry Jones said after the game. "They took advantage of their knowledge of us."

Payton spread the Cowboys out on defense, and Gibbs forced Romo to stay in the pocket on offense.

(opposite) After three years on Parcell's staff in Dallas, Payton knew exactly how to stop Romo and the Cowboys.

Up until that game, Romo's most effective plays had come when he moved around the pocket and improvised to make a play when there shouldn't have been one. Against the Saints, they forced him to be still. The game was, in effect, this first time Romo had been knocked down.

"I think that would not only fit him," Parcells said. "We took another one on the chin. I'm anxious to see how we respond."

Romo and the Cowboys would respond favorably ... at least for a week.

Week 15: at Atlanta, December 16, 2006

The loss against the Saints was the evidence for Parcells to remind his offense coaches that Romo, despite his success, wasn't a 10-year veteran. He hadn't started 10 NFL games yet. At one point during the game against the Saints, NBC color analyst John Madden said he thought the Cowboys were asking Romo to do too much. The head coach agreed. "It's, 'Hey, let's take a look at this and let's not get too far off the reservation ourselves,'" Parcells said the day after the loss against the Saints.

Nearly everything the Cowboys couldn't do against the Saints they could against the Falcons in a game televised by the NFL Network on a Saturday night in Atlanta at the Georgia Dome. It helped that the Falcons teetered on the edge of a losing season, after which head coach Jim Mora Jr. would be fired.

The game began well enough. Late in the first quarter, Romo had the Cowboys at the Falcons' 7-yard line. In a year where Owens would lead the world in dropped passes with 17, he made one of the best catches of the season when he trapped a Romo pass with one arm against his body despite tight coverage for a 7-0 lead.

With the game tied at 14 late in the first half, Romo uncorked one of those highlight throws that is replayed ad nauseam. On a play-action pass, Romo had plenty of time before throwing a deep pass down the left sideline where a streaking Owens beat a pair of defenders for a 51-yard touchdown. Romo sprinted to the end zone to celebrate with Owens, and the Cowboys led, 21-14.

There was the infectious enthusiasm from the same guy who as an eighth-grader wrote on a football, "I play for the love of the game."

The plan to rely on Romo less wasn't working. The defense was demonstrating the uncanny ability to stop no one. And when Falcons fullback Justin Griffith caught his second touchdown of the night early in the third quarter, the Falcons had a 28-21 lead. Romo was going to have to play more like the 10-year veteran he wasn't.

The defense actually held the Falcons the remainder of the game, and Romo put together touchdown drives of 66 and 80 yards in the second half to win going away, 38-28. Romo passed for 278 yards with two touchdowns.

The Cowboys were 9-5, atop the NFC East, and

(opposite) Romo and the Cowboys would struggle early in the game in Atlanta, but they would rally for some big plays and win by 10 to take control of the NFC East.

in the playoffs for the first time in two years. They had an outside chance of earning a first round bye in the playoffs. A few days later, Romo was named to the Pro Bowl roster.

"Am I surprised? I don't think that would be a strong enough word," Parcells said. "But other than that I have nothing else to say about it."

Christmas was a few days away.

Week 16: vs. Philadelphia, December 25, 2006

Because the Cowboys are as big as any team in the North America, they are often picked to play the headline game as often as the NFL will allow. With Romo at quarterback, the TV networks wanted the Cowboys as often as possible. Before Romo played, the most interesting development was the old-school Parcells clashing with Terrell Owens.

But they never had a genuine clash. They opted for the passive-aggressive jabs the way neighbors may fight. For the most part, Parcells ignored Owens, as did the rest of his team. The only time Owens made for can't-miss television viewing was his first return to Philadelphia, and that was back in early October. That game itself – a 38-24 Eagles win – was more dramatic than anything Owens did on the sidelines.

As it turned out, Owens/Eagles or Owens/Parcells never made for the must-see TV the way a producer might hope. It was too scripted and too forced. Romo, however, was must-see. He was the ultimate greeting card. The genuine Boy Scout done good.

Tom Brady had at least played at Michigan, and was at least drafted. Romo's story was better. So NBC lined up the maximum number of games the league would allow.

Then, before Cowboys/Eagles II, a gift – there on the field was the cute little long-haired blonde straight from reality TV, Carrie Underwood. And she was hugging Romo.

The star of American Idol had replaced Jessica Simpson as the Romo's arm candy. Actually, Simpson was more of an *Us Weekly* style rumor than reality. Turns out, the Dallas-native Simpson never was the heartthrob for Romo that was reported. Her dad, however, was a big Cowboys fan. He was looking for tickets.

Underwood apparently was more serious than a ticket seeker. She, like Romo, enjoyed similar immediate fame after spending the majority of time trying to escape obscurity. She was "with" Romo, and she sat in Jerry Jones' suite during the game. She was a genuine, celebrity straight from TV and the gossip pages. Gossip websites such as PerezHilton.com and others threw up pictures of the two on their sites as quickly as possible.

Cowboys/Eagles II on Christmas Day at Texas Stadium suddenly jumped from the sports pages to the life and arts section, too.

A game that once looked so watchable when the schedule was released in the offseason had turned to a late-season dog when quarterback Donovan

(opposite) Suddenly Romo was living a charmed life on the field and off, as he was soon seen in the arm of American Idol star Carrie Underwood.

McNabb suffered a season-ending injury on Nov. 19. His replacement, veteran Jeff Garcia, stepped in and in his first game lost, dropping the Eagles record to 5-6. They were dead.

But, like the Cowboys, the Eagles were actually better with their undrafted backup quarterback, Jeff Garcia. By the time they came into Texas Stadium on a pleasant holiday afternoon, they were 8-6 and had the chance to re-take the lead in the NFC East. If the Cowboys won, they would claim their first divisional title since 1998.

It wasn't close. The Eagles won, 23-7. Garcia and the Eagles were everything Romo and the Cowboys weren't.

The Eagles led 7-0 after a long drive, and it was happening again. The Cowboys defense could stop no one. The team was forced to rely on Romo.

It might have worked, too. But early in the second quarter, the Cowboys were at the Eagles' 1-yard line with a chance to tie the game. Parcells opted to go for it on fourth down. But Marion Barber was stopped for a 3-yard loss. No one could have guessed that play effectively ended the game.

Romo kept it close, and the Cowboys only trailed 10-7 at the half, but it felt like 30. They wouldn't score again. The Eagles rushed for 204 yards, the most by a Cowboys opponent at Texas Stadium since 2000.

For the first time in his brief career as a starter, Romo looked the part of a rookie quarterback. In four drives in the second half, he was sacked twice, and threw two interceptions. For the second time in three games, he completed less than 50 percent of his passes, and he threw for a meager 142 yards. A Cowboys offense that averaged 25 points in Romo's first eight starts was effectively neutered by the Eagles.

As good as Romo was, he was beginning to show signs that he hadn't played very much. The league was figuring out Tony Romo. For all of his preparation, there were still some things he had never seen before. "That one corner blitz Philly put on? He had never seen that. Ever," Ramiro Romo said. "If he says he did – nah, nah, nah. He never saw that guy coming. He is seeing stuff he's never seen before. He's getting the whole perspective."

Using his best Parcells-isms, Romo said after the game, "You are what you are in this league. We'll find out when we get into the tournament." Tournament was Parcells speak for playoffs. And speaking of the tournament, the Cowboys chances were looking bleaker with every down they played.

First round bye? Bye.

NFC East title? Nope.

Home playoff game? Maybe.

Momentum? Yeah, he left, too.

And confidence? Fading.

"Unthinkable. Unthinkable. I'm disappointed for our fans," Jerry Jones said after the game. "It's a complete organizational failure in my mind."

The Cowboys were 9-6. But they had the Lions –

(opposite) The Christmas Day clash with the Eagles would see the Cowboys battered by a physical Philadelphia team on both sides of the ball.

arguably the worst team in the history of organized sports – coming to Texas Stadium for the season finale on New Year's Eve Day.

Week 17: vs. Detroit, December 31, 2006

The best way to describe the Lions during the 2006 season? They sucked. They were the NFL's version of the Homecoming opponent. They were 2-13 when they came to Texas Stadium for the rare noon kickoff on New Year's Eve. Whatever problems dogged the Cowboys, which one needed all of their fingers and toes to track at this point, the Lions would rectify.

Six seconds into the game, Cowboys safety Roy Williams intercepted a Lions quarterback Jon Kitna pass and returned it 51 yards for a touchdown. The Cowboys might not be the eventual Super Bowl champion, but this game was proof they were not the bunch that was outscored by the combined total of 68-24 in their past two home games. As it turns out, they were worse. Williams' interception was nullified by a penalty.

The Lions led 20-14 at the half. This was worse than the Saints game. Or the Eagles game. Those teams were going to the playoffs. But the Lions? This was a team with an express ticket to the top of the NFL draft every April. These same Lions led 30-24 at the end of three quarters.

It didn't last too long; Romo pulled out one of those plays he would eventually make more famous.

Facing a 3rd-and-3 from his own 3-yard line, Romo was preparing to throw him from his own end zone when he dropped the ball. As the ball bounced around, he grabbed it, narrowly escaped a defender, and flipped the pass to Terrell Owens at the 14-yard line for a first down. Two plays later, Romo hooked up with Owens on a 56-yard touchdown to take a 31-30 lead in the fourth quarter.

They coughed up the lead, again, but Romo was back in position to play the part of hero. Romo and the Cowboys started their final drive at their own 35-yard line with 2:58 remaining and one timeout. Romo moved the Cowboys to the Lions' 10-yard line with 41 seconds remaining.

He had three chances from the 6-yard line to try to put his team in a position to tie. On fourth down, the Texas Stadium crowd felt more sick than nervous. Even if the Cowboys won, it didn't matter. Beating the Lions in overtime, which is what it would likely require, wasn't an encouraging sign for a team that needed some sign confidence. Romo was forced to scramble on the final meaningful play, and he was stopped at the 2-yard line.

Detroit 39. Dallas 31. The Lions hadn't scored that many points since 2003.

Romo finished 23-of-32 for 321 yards with two touchdowns, one interception and two fumbles.

Why could this team think it could win a Super Bowl?

"That's a stumper," defensive back Terence

(opposite) Towards the end of the 2006 season some of the luster had dulled as Romo began looking more like the first-year starter that he was.

Newman said.

The Cowboys finished the season 9-7. They lost three of their last four games, all at home. "It's very frustrating and disappointing for me," Romo said after the game. "It's one of those weeks where I'm going to have to let it go today when I get out of here."

This game would be much easier to get over than what was about to happen.

NFC Playoffs, Wild Card Weekend at Seattle, January 6, 2007

Romo stood in his locker in front of a small handful of reporters in early December when someone asked him if he'd like to drop his title as the team's holder for kicks. "I'd like to," he said.

But holding for a field goal was the last thing anybody in the franchise was worried about the week of the Cowboys' game against defending NFC champion Seahawks in Seattle. Their main concerns was a defense that had collapsed. "If we had the answers I swear we would try to correct it," linebacker Bradie James said of a defense that allowed 132 points in their final four games. They gave up the same amount in the previous eight games.

Parcells still felt he had a good team. He reminded them collectively, "Don't be the one to send us home." It wasn't a scare tactic; it was a reminder to focus.

But there were concerns about the quarterback who look exposed, or at least inexperienced. In Romo's last five regular season starts, he was intercepted eight times and lost two fumbles. In his first five starts, he had two interceptions and lost one fumble. His mechanics looked off. "I'm not saying Romo fell down," NBC analyst John Madden said the week of the game on a conference call. "When you play a young quarterback, you're going to have an inconsistent offense."

It was the exact kind of development Parcells feared, and warned fans and the media about. Romo had begun to be a little careless with the ball. In his attempt to make the big play, he had thrown away the safe play.

"You guys were laughing at me that it's a little less than perfect," Parcells said of Romo a few days before the playoff game. "I think that's what you witness what you were talking about. It's come to fruition. He was getting away with things and now he didn't get away with them quite as much."

First-year quarterbacks coach Chris Palmer, who was essentially hired in the offseason to work with Drew Bledsoe, had told David Lee to no longer speak to Romo earlier in December. As a result, Lee would have to often write notes and leave them for Romo in the team's lunch room; mostly, they were suggestions about his mechanics. The week of the playoffs, Parcells asked that Lee begin to coach Romo again, specifically to work on those mechanics.

The Cowboys were going to the playoffs against a team with a secondary that was both bad and

(opposite) The Cowboys would stumble into the 2006 playoffs after losing three of their last four games – all at home.

depleted by injury. Their starting cornerbacks were out with injuries, and they had to move safety Kelly Herndon to cornerback. They signed Pete Hunter to the team a few days before the game, and he had been a loan officer living not far from the Cowboys' practice facility when he received the call.

Even against the Seattle secondary, the playoffs were a struggle for Romo. But the Cowboys took a 10-6 lead at the half after Romo found Patrick Crayton for a 13-yard touchdown with 18 seconds remaining in the first half. Romo wasn't good, but his team was winning.

The Cowboys led 20-13, mostly thanks to rookie returner Miles Austin's 93-yard kickoff return for a touchdown in the third quarter. But then the really strange things began to happen in the fourth quarter.

The Cowboys stopped the Seahawks on a 4th-and-2 at their own 2-yard line with 6:48 remaining. On the following play, receiver Terry Glenn lost a fumble that was ruled a safety.

The Seahawks led 21-20, but all would be forgiven if Romo could lead the Cowboys to a field goal, maybe even a touchdown, to win the game. All he had to do was show the fourth-quarter flair he had shown before.

Starting at his own 28-yard line with 4:18 remaining, he was suddenly the passer he had not been in the first three quarters. An 11-yard pass to Crayton. A 12-yard pass to Terrell Owens. And then running back Julius Jones sprang loose for a 35-yard gain on

a draw. There was that flair, and the Cowboys were going to win.

With less than two minutes remaining in the game, Romo completed what appeared to be a first-down pass to tight end Jason Witten to the Seattle 1-yard line. But after an instant replay, the ball was spotted at the 2-yard line with 1:19 remaining.

Romo stayed on the field to hold. Kicker Martin Gramatica trotted out for a 19-yard field goal, less than the distance of an extra point.

The snap was clean, and Romo caught the ball. But then it slipped out of his hands as he tried to place it. Hell broke loose. He immediately grabbed the ball, and began running towards the left side. It was a microcosm of the entire season: Tony Romo was going to take the sure thing that had gone terribly wrong and right it.

Of course, that didn't happen. Seahawks safety Jordin Babineaux chased Romo down from behind and tripped him at the 2-yard line. Romo was one yard short from a first down, and two yards from a touchdown.

"You gotta be kidding me?" Cowboys special teams coach Bruce DeHaven said to himself. "I'm worried about getting the kick off. I'm not worried about getting the field goal off. I've got a good holder, and a good snapper. Those two are the last things I'm worried about. We're right there, point blank. We had a lot of chances to win that game. A lot. But when things happen at the end, it gets

(opposite) The bobbled snap was a disaster for Romo and the Cowboys, whose giddy late season run met a crushing end in the playoffs against Seattle.

pinned on those plays."

The Seahawks celebrated and Qwest Field shook. Nine of the 11 Cowboys players on the field returned to the sidelines. Center Al Johnson was one of the two to stay. The other was Romo, who sat on the goal line clutching his face mask with both hands.

"Are you OK?" Johnson screamed so Romo could hear him.

Physically, Romo was OK. Emotionally he wasn't.

"He was pretty devastated," Johnson said.

Romo returned to the sideline and stared off into the distance by himself on the bench. He would throw one more pass that night – a heave from midfield on the game's final play – that fell incomplete in the endzone. Romo's "first" season was over.

The Cowboys' locker room was mostly silent. As players showered and dressed, Romo stayed in his stall facing his locker, and the floor. It appeared as if he was crying. Terrell Owens walked over and tried to encourage Romo. The Cowboys finished 9-8; another playoff team evicted early.

"As I tried to tell Tony, not to get down on yourself, things happen for a reason," Owens said. "It just wasn't really meant to be. If you give Tony nine times out of 10, he will put that ball down."

Nine out of 10? It had never happened before.

Parcells addressed the media as the head coach of the Dallas Cowboys for the final time. He would officially retire from football on January 23.

Romo went to the media podium, the streaks of tears still apparent on his face. Regardless if you were a Cowboy lover or hater, a Romo fan or loyal to Drew Bledsoe, it was impossible not to feel for Tony Romo at that moment in time. His was the face of genuine pain and hurt. "For it to end like that, and for me to be the cause of it is tough," Romo said. "I don't know if I ever felt this low at any point."

Romo went to the team bus where, as always, he took his seat across from special teams coach Bruce DeHaven. "Everybody was crushed," DeHaven said. "Nobody said a word."

When Romo boarded the team plane, he was the first person on. The next person to board was quarterbacks coach David Lee, who walked over to Romo.

"No. 1, we're not here if it's not for you and what you did," Lee told Romo. "This is one of those hurdles you've gotta clear to get this franchise to the Super Bowl."

Romo then pulled out another Parcells-ism. The same one Parcells used on his players earlier in the week.

"I'm the reason we went home," Romo said. "I'm the reason we went home."

The great sports story now had its tragedy.

It just wasn't the end of the story. ■

(opposite) Though the national media wondered if he would ever recover from the botched snap fiasco, Romo stayed focused on the big picture.

Chapter VI

The Answer

Romo quickly bounced back from the botched snap

The next morning after the playoff loss in Seattle, Tony Romo looked like had hadn't slept, and he sounded just as bad and dispirited as he did in the press conference after the game. By that point in the morning, about 10 a.m., word was spreading around the NFL that the ball Romo lost control of was directly out of the box. The rules said Romo should have used a broken-in football, not the piece of ice he did.

"Yeah it was slick ... it doesn't matter. I should have gotten it down," he said.

A few months later, the NFL would change the rules to make sure that if such a play happened again, it wouldn't be the fault of the equipment. It's known as the Romo Rule. But what did that matter now? The Cowboys' season was over, and Romo faced an offseason of doubt.

Inside the coaches' offices the playoff loss was being graded, reviewed and evaluated by the staff. "That game may be a black mark on Tony Romo for the rest of his career," one offensive assistant said aloud in the meeting. "He may never get over that."

Neither Lee nor Parcells bought that. Before he left, he talked to Romo a few times. One of the basic problems with Romo was the very aspect that coaches loved about him: intelligence. Romo can usually quickly figure out where a conversation was going, which is good, and bad. Those people don't always listen to every single word. So Parcells would have to remind him of certain things.

No. 1: Romo didn't lose that game. After Romo lost the ball at the 2-yard line, the Cowboys still had three timeouts, and there was 1:14 remaining. But on first down, Seahawks running back Shaun Alexander ripped his lone big carry of the game, a 22-yarder. Had the Cowboys held the Seahawks to without a first down, they would have likely punted near their own end zone with about one minute remaining. As it was, by the time the Cowboys got the ball back, there were two seconds left and the ball was at midfield.

(opposite) Like any great athlete, Romo has shown the ability to bounce back from his disappointments.

No. 2: Romo was going to be fine if he just settled down and played the game.

No. 3: He was pulling for him.

Parcells would leave less than two weeks later. Romo would have a new coach in the coming weeks – Wade Phillips. But over the coming months interest increased in both Tony Romo the player, and Tony Romo the celebrity.

Immediately after "The Bobble" a great deal of speculation was raised that Romo would never be the same again. That play would have a Bill Buckner type of impact; that Romo would never be the same mentally again as a result of a split-second moment in Seattle. For the time being, he became a punchline. On eBay, a six-inch plastic figurine of his bobble was being sold; at one point, the bidding reached $250. Romo eventually split for Colorado to ski with his friends.

But Tony Romo was still a Pro Bowler. Unlike some of the invitees, Romo wanted to play in this game, and not just because the game was in Hawaii. He wanted to finish the 2006 season on a different note than he had in Seattle. He even asked NFC coach Sean Payton to let him hold on extra points and field goals.

Romo entered the game early in the second half for the NFC. But his second pass was intercepted by Ravens' safety Ed Reed. Early in the fourth quarter, Romo was sacked on a 4th-and-5 at the AFC's 16-yard line. It got worse. Romo had the NFC at the AFC 1-yard line with 5:07 remaining in the game, but he was stopped. Now Romo really was pulling off the impossible – he was jeered by some of the fans in the Pro Bowl. But Romo showed his fourth quarter flair, and led the NFC back from a 14-point hole. He cut the deficit to two points with 1:58 remaining when he completed a 47-yard touchdown pass to Cardinals receiver Anquan Boldin. The NFC eventually lost on a last-second field goal, 31-28. But Romo had finished his first season as a starting quarterback with something other than a bobble.

The offseason had officially started. And Romo wasted no time in taking full advantage of being the quarterback of America's Team.

Two days after the Pro Bowl, he was spotted at the Key Club on the Sunset Strip in Los Angeles. The musical comedy act cover band "Metal Skool" begged for Romo to come on stage. He helped sing Journey's "Don't Stop Believing." Less than 24 hours later, You Tube had the video on its site. The video confirms what his family, friends, teammates already know: Tono Romo can't sing. Dogs in greater Los Angeles reportedly complained about the performance. "He can't carry a tune, bless his heart," Ramiro said of his son. "He's totally tone deaf."

By early March, rumors had taken off that his relationship with budding country signing star Carrie Underwood were cruising at 35,000 feet. They were spotted at each other's birthday parties.

Then his day job got in the way of Romo's bur-

(opposite) Romo's ability to stay grounded and keep things in perspective was apparent to all during his Pro Bowl appearance.

geoning celebrity status. Draft day, 2008. Rated as one of the best quarterbacks or players in the class was Notre Dame's Brady Quinn. He was expected to go in the top six or seven picks, and no lower than eighth. But Quinn began to drop, and it quickly became obvious the Cowboys could have him with the 22nd pick in the first round. The Cowboys rated Quinn as the eighth-best prospect in the draft class. At the very least, they could select Quinn for insurance just in case Romo was the player of December and not November.

But there are two draft boards for every team. There is the Quarterback Board, and the Everybody Else Board. The Cowboys didn't need to go to the Quarterback Board, so they passed. They traded that pick to the Browns for their first round pick in 2008. Tony Romo was indeed The Man. "It would be the Drew Henson thing all over again," Romo said. "You have to win the job, perform and be good. Either you're good enough or you're not."

Cowboys owner Jerry Jones said both he and new head coach Wade Phillips thought about Quinn, "But we just thought that the best way to get to the Super Bowl is with Tony Romo as our quarterback."

It was done. But Tony Romo's Summer of Fun wasn't. He made a run at qualifying for the U.S. Open in early May, but didn't make the cut.

About one week later, there was Romo on national TV again, and he was hard to miss. He was Underwood's official purse holder when she was

called to the stage accept one her three Country Music Awards in Las Vegas. And to finish off the month of May, there was Romo's big grin in Mexico City – as a judge for the Miss Universe pageant. To complete the summer, he played in The American Century Celebrity Golf Championship in Lake Tahoe. These events are usually reserved for either very good golfers who were athletes, or just big names. Names such as Mario Lemieux, John Elway and Charles Barkley. Romo finished 11th.

By the time the Cowboys began their training camp in San Antonio, most of the Tony Romo-talk was about his off-the-field performance. Indeed, he enjoyed what being a celebrity brings in this country – priority seating, plenty of adulation, lots of free stuff, and a wide selection from the pretty people table, too.

Romo kept a different perspective on it, or at least he tried.

"I really don't know what that is," he said when asked if it was that big deal of a deal to be the quarterback of America's Team. "I'm lucky to be blessed and good at something that I enjoy in life. As far as it being taken away, I'd still be happy being the club pro in Burlington, Wisconsin. As far as the enjoyment factor, it adds something to it. It's a neat thing and it's special to be a part of. But I don't look at it in the third-person, or far afar, like 'It's exciting' and all that stuff. It is exciting, but it seems normal."

This part of his life was possible because he is the

(opposite) With an off-season to digest all he had accomplished, Romo charged into the 2007 season determined to lead the Cowboys to victory.

starter for the Dallas Cowboys. A backup doesn't film commericals, date music stars, shoot ESPN spots or receive an invite for celebrity golf tournaments. All of these off-the-field possibilities were possible because of what he did on the field in Dallas.

When the Cowboys began training camp in San Antonio in late July of 2007, bobble talk was dead. It wasn't an easy thing to move past, but eventually Romo reached closure. At some point, thinking about it any more wasn't going to do any good. A bobble wasn't going to be the reason he was not a good NFL quarterback.

"[I got over it] after a while," Romo said in May of 2007. "You go on and you get up and say, 'It's time to win some more football games.' After 10 years from now, we'll see how my career turns out."

By the end of training camp, Romo had proven he was an NFL player. The Cowboys signed veteran Brad Johnson to be his backup. For the first time since his junior season at Eastern Illinois, Tony Romo had no competition to be his team's starting quarterback. What no one knew was, how good was he? Was he the star from November 2006? Was he the falling star of December 2006? Was he destined to be a bus driver? Or was he a quarterback in the process of coming down because the league had figured him out? No one knew.

Week 1: vs. New York Giants, September 9, 2007
Even though the Cowboys weren't the defending Super Bowl champs, they were the A-list team for TV networks. When the schedule was released, the Cowboys had the maximum number of appearances on NBC, and night games scheduled. They were initially scheduled to play in 11 games that would be the feature attraction.

A lot of that is the power of America's Team. Some of it had to do with Tony Romo, who led his team on Sunday Night Football against the New York Giants, and quarterback Eli Manning.

Manning and Romo couldn't be more opposite. Manning is from the finest breed of quarterback blood – father Archie and big brother Peyton are icons. Eli went to Ole Miss, just like his father, was the first pick in the 2004 draft, and engineered a draft day trade from the Chargers to the Giants. His bloodlines screamed star.

But there was Romo, who for the second time in as many starts against Baby Eli out-played him, and won. Romo threw for 345 yards passing with four touchdowns as the Cowboys won, 45-35. Every time the Giants got close, Romo diced the Giants again. And again. And again.

Romo was calmer and more confident in the huddle. He was on a different level with his receivers, too. Late in the fourth quarter and the Giants trailing 38-35, Romo bent over in the huddle. "Look for the sight," Romo told second-year receiver Sam Hurd.

That meant if Hurd saw the safety begin to show a blitz, he would run to a hole about 7 yards deep.

(opposite) A new, calmer Romo was calling the shots in 2007.

AP/ Wide World

Both Hurd and Romo saw it, and "That pass was perfect. You couldn't beat it," Hurd said of Romo's pass that he took 51-yards for the final touchdown.

"Going in we didn't know what to expect," Romo said after a performance that would earn him NFC Offensive Player of the Week honors; he also improved to 3-0 in starts against quarterbacks named Manning. "There is not a lot to go by.... I don't think you're going to put up this many points every week. That's unrealistic."

It was unrealistic, but after that game scoring 45 points every week looked entirely possible.

Week 2: at Miami Dolphins, September 16, 2007

By now Romo had shown he had "It." No one can define what "It" is, but all of the great performers have it.

"'It' means you just find a way," he said. "You are good enough to figure it out in some way shape or form."

"It" can't be coached, either. A player has "it" or he does not. Some of "it" is instincts combined with athleticism combined with an innate sense of timing. And some of "it" is trusting himself to make a play when it is there, and when it is not. Romo had to do both on a sweltering afternoon in South Florida against a Dolphins that was in the process of heading to the top of the 2008 draft board.

The Cowboys actually trailed with less than 10 minutes remaining in the third quarter, 13-10. Romo then used a short field and moved the Cowboys to the Dolphins' 2-yard line. Then "It" came out.

After a quick fake handoff, Romo was supposed to run a naked bootleg to his right. But Dolphins linebacker Joey Porter read the play, and was immediately on Romo and wrapped his arms around him at the 6-yard line. Romo was on his way down when Dolphins defensive end Matt Roth came flying towards his body. All of a sudden, Romo threw ball into the end zone for tight end Tony Curtis, who caught it for his first career NFL catch. "I didn't know Tony was going to be there," Romo said. "It wasn't something, 'Like, please turn!' That would have made it easier. I was going down and it was like, 'Is there anyway I can get out of this?'"

The play was dead, but Romo made it breathe. "I didn't think he was going to throw it to me," Curtis said. "I didn't know how he could. I didn't think I was open. I'm the third option on that play."

Late in the fourth quarter, the Cowboys had the chance to bury the Dolphins. Facing a 4th-and-5 from the Miami 35-yard line and 4:08 remaining, the Cowboys could have tried a long field goal. Maybe a punt. Or go for it. They chose Door No. 3. Romo threw a deep strike down the left sideline for Terrell Owens and a touchdown.

Part of the "It" is ignoring the gravity of the moment around you. To Romo, it really is just a football game. Nothing else. Late in the game during a timeout, the same song that was used to intro-

(opposite) Just like in many games before, Romo's skill and luck with improvising would help his team against the Dolphins.

duce wrestler Hulk Hogan blarred over the stadium speakers. And Romo was signing right along with it, at the top of his lungs.

"Joey Porter and (Dolphins defensive end) Jason Taylor are looking at me, and I'm like, 'I'm sorry. This is how he is,'" tight end Anthony Fasano said. "He sings Vanilla Ice, all of that stuff during the game. At the top of his lungs. It's not funny."

Romo did not post an offensive player of the week performance – 14-of-29 passing for 186 yards and two touchdowns – but he was good when it mattered. And the Cowboys won 37-20.

By the end of the game, the Dolphins were beginning to agree with the rest of the league when Taylor said of Romo, "He's a very good quarterback."

Week 3: at Chicago Bears, September 23, 2007

Romo and the Cowboys were making their second appearance on NBC in three weeks. This time, against the defending NFC champion Bears in Soldier Field, and specifically against the greatest defense God himself could design ... or something like that.

David Haugh of the *Chicago Tribune* wrote the day before the game, "In Tony Romo's first 13 NFL starts, he has faced one top-10 defense. His 14th Sunday at Soldier Field will come against the Bears' fifth-ranked unit. Romo will encounter the quickest, meanest group of men who ever have chased him around a professional football field.

Romo's college degree might be from Eastern Illinois University, but he could get an NFL education in crisis management from the Bears defense. He has started against 13 defenses whose average rank is No. 22. Six of those defenses were ranked 25th or lower."

All statements were true. But "I'm a wiley vet," Romo said sarcastically the week of that game. That comment was Romo. Very few things weren't above a subtle joke or jab.

No, Romo probably hadn't seen a defense like the Bears. On the Cowboys' first offensive play, it looked like it, too. Romo was sacked for an 11-yard loss. On the next drive, he threw an interception. The Bears defense was making Romo look more like Rex Grossman than Rex Grossman, and the game was tied at three at the half.

The third quarter was different. Romo began to pass his way all over the Bears' defense, and the Cowboys took a 10-3 lead when he found tight end Jason Witten on a 3-yard pass in the endzone. By the middle of the fourth quarter, the Monsters were being shredded in their own Midway. By the end of the game, Romo was on the sidelines watching Brad Johnson take the snaps. The Cowboys won 34-10; they out-scored the Bears 31-7 in the second half. Romo threw for 329 yards with a pair of touchdowns.

The Cowboys were 3-0; so much for the highly ranked defense theory.

(opposite) Against the vaunted Bears defense and in front of a national audience, Romo turned in one of the best performances of his young career.

Week 4: St. Louis Rams, September 30, 2007

It wasn't until this game Tony Romo was officially compared to one of his predecessors. But near the end of the first half, there was Roger Staubach running again on the Texas Stadium field.

He wasn't, of course, but for one 30-second glimpse Captain America admitted he caught shades of himself.

The Cowboys were tied with the winless Rams at seven. When Romo lined up in the shotgun with 56 seconds remaining before half time, the game had no life. The fans were bored. The team looked bored, too. The Cowboys faced a 3rd-and-3 at the 50-yard line, and teetered on the edge of keeping the Rams in the game. What happened next became an instant classic, both for the Cowboys, but specifically for Romo.

Center Andre Gurode snapped the ball over Romo's head.

"Fall on it! Fall on it!" Gurode said to himself.

Romo turned around and immediately began to run back for the ball as a pair of Rams defenders chased him. He finally caught up to the bouncing ball at the 26-yard line, but it came up into his stomach and immediately bounced backwards some more. Romo finally grabbed the ball at his own 16-yard line and immediately turned around and began to run away from the two defenders. He pump-faked one Rams defender at the 26-yard line, and kept running up the left sideline before he ran out of bounds at the Rams' 46-yard line.

"When he got the ball and started running I thought, 'This could work,'" Gurode said.

Statistically, the run gained four yards. But Romo had actually run 76 yards.

Here is the call from Fox play-by-play announcer Joe Buck: "The snap over the head of Romo, and now it's a footrace. Romo can't get on top of it, finally does. Will try and make something happen. Tony Romo ... doing his thing. First down Dallas. Unbelievable."

It was appropriate that Buck's broadcast partner is former Cowboys quarterback Troy Aikman. "You don't think they'll be showing this clip for years, do you?" Aikman asked as the replay rolled on the telecast.

"The legend just grew," Buck said.

Cowboys coach Wade Phillips was on the opposite sideline when Romo ran, and after the game he uttered the magic words, "It reminded me of Staubach.... I saw him do it before. It wasn't for a score but he ran around long enough to complete a pass for the first down. It was a miracle play, but it did remind me of Staubach. Staubach is right — (Romo) does look like him."

Staubach watched the play in amazement. He said he wasn't sure people would realize just how hard a play like that was. Just to gather the ball and continue to run is hard enough. It was the type of play that his coach, Tom Landry, tried in vain to get him to stop.

(opposite) The game against St. Louis would provide Romo with one of the signature moments of his young career.

And the play reminded him of a conversation he had with Romo in the previous fall. "Don't let them coach that out of you," Staubach told Romo.

A Texas Stadium crowd that to that point was mostly irritated at the closeness of the score was not only alive, but screaming. The stadium jumped. The players beamed with grins. Video game players couldn't do this. The Rams defensive players were frustrated, and exhausted. "And in the blink of an eye – I don't know if he broke cotain or what, next thing you know, he's running down field," Rams defensive tackle La'Roi Glover said.

This is Tony Romo. The same Romo that made plays up on Dinty Moore field in Burlington, or at Eastern Illinois. Texas Stadium may be bigger, but the field is his glorified playground. "I was thinking, 'Don't give up a touchdown and don't get killed,'" Romo said. "Once you pick up the ball, you try to make a play." Five plays later, he dropped back to pass; nothing was open, so he ran in for the touchdown from 15 yards away. The Cowboys led 14-7 at the half.

The Cowboys won 35-7, and Romo passed for 339 yards and accounted for four touchdowns. But all anybody wanted to talk about was his "4-yard" run.

"Oh, that was the play that won the game," Romo said rolling his eyes and smiling in the post-game press conference.

He was only joking, but he was probably right. And so was Buck – the legend just grew.

Week 5: at Buffalo Bills, October 8, 2007

This was the game Bill Parcells always feared when he coached Romo. The 4-0 Cowboys were a 10-point favorite against a team crushed by injury, and starting quarterback making his second career start.

But on a frenzied night in Buffalo, for the first time in his NFL career, Tony Romo was historically awful. It may have also been his most impressive game to date. The awfulness started early, too. Romo's first two passes and they were both intercepted, and one was returned for a touchdown. Not to worry, the night was about to get worse.

Trailing 10-7, Romo threw a pass from his own 5-yard line when Bills' defensive end Chris Kelsay batted the ball in the air, looked up and ran a few steps forward before he caught the ball in the endzone. The Bills were leading 17-7, and Romo's passes had led to two Buffalo touchdowns.

As bad as Romo was, he didn't stop trying, playing, and throwing. The Cowboys trailed 17-13 early in the second half. But then Bills' returner Terrence McGee returned the ensuing kick 103 yards for a touchdown.

Trailing by eight, and Romo had the chance to tie the game with 11:18 remaining. But on a scramble attempt up the middle, the ball was stripped by Bills defensive end Aaron Schobel and Buffalo recovered. "I'm sure they were pissed," Romo said after the game of his teammates.

(opposite) Romo would be historically awful against Buffalo, but he wouldn't let it get him down for long.

He was right. They were pissed. At this point, Cowboys linebacker Bradie James popped. He screamed and yelled in the direction of the offense as it collectively walked off the field after Romo's fumble. "I don't know what I was trying to do," James said. "You can't go by like nothing has happened. That's all it was."

But the defense put Romo again position to tie the game at 24.

"You guys think you can go on three?" Romo asked his team in the huddle about the snap count.

"Romo, are you crazy?" receiver Patrick Crayton said.

Crazy? No. Kidding? Yes. Romo may have been awful, but he hadn't lost his sense of humor. Then he promptly forced a pass to a triple-covered Jason Witten at the goal line for yet another interception.

This is what Parcells feared about Romo. That the young quarterback was prone to the temptation of going for the big play instead of the easy play. A lot of quarterbacks fall into it – Brett Favre, Drew Bledsoe, etc. It's not an easy thing to let go of, especially when you've had a rotten night. The player wants to make up for his mistakes by being spectacular on the next pass.

Then Romo summoned his fourth-quarter flair again to redeem himself. Crayton caught a 4-yard touchdown pass from Romo with 24 seconds remaining. But Owens was unable to catch the 2-point conversion. The comeback wasn't to be. They didn't deserve it – they were minus-5 in turnovers.

But then a football miracle happened when they recovered the onside kick. Romo could still win despite the most awful peformance of his career. The "It" was still there. After an Owens' drop, Romo completed his next two passes to the Bills' 35-yard line with two seconds remaining.

Romo had done what he could. It was up to the rookie kicker, Nick Folk to try a career-long 53-yard field goal. He nailed it, but the kick was waved off because of a Bills' timeout. Kick No. 2 was just as good, and the Cowboys won 25-24.

"I've never seen anything like that," Owens said after the game.

Tony Romo's line read: 29-of-50, 309 yards, two touchdowns, one lost fumble, and five interceptions. "Well, he didn't throw six," coach Wade Phillips joked after the game.

Romo also had one massive win.

So who could say this coming?

"I'd be lying if I said I knew he was going to do what he is doing," said former Cowboys scout Jim Hess, who was instrumental in bringing Romo to Dallas. "I knew he had the potential. The Brett Favre-type of thing. But this? Give Parcells some credit – and I don't like to do that very often – but I think once we had him he saw what Sean Payton and I had. And, maybe he was desperate. I don't know.

"I guess the thing that maybe is surprising is that

(opposite) Despite five interceptions, Romo would throw for over 300 yards and the Cowboys would win in the waning seconds in Buffalo.

maybe he's got a lot more talent than anyone is giving him credit for. We may just have to admit he has really good talent. He has more than I realized."

There's one who didn't see it.

"Well, he's the exception to the rule. And probably a little more so at quarterback than some other positions," Sean Payton said. "He was at the combine for four days, so everyone had plenty chance to see him. And you never know how far progress is going to take him. You knew he had some ability, and he's worked hard to get where he's at now. I've got a lot of good Tony Romo stories, but I'm happy for him. He's playing well, the team's playing well, and they believe in him. He's a good leader, too."

How about Bill Parcells?

"I would say that would be a reach," he said.

Tony Romo, the player that no Division I program wanted, and the one I-AA program that did offered only a partial scholarship.

Tony Romo, the player 32 NFL teams passed on the draft seven times each.

Tony Romo ... America's Next Quarterback. ∎

(opposite) His rise has been meteoric, but Romo will have to continue to turn in signature performances to keep his team on top. (above) Romo and Jones are all smiles after Romo signed a contract that pays him $67.5 million through 2013.

Epilogue

Jones locked up Romo through 2013 with a $67.5 million contract

This story is still chapters away from its conclusion. Even though he started relatively late by NFL standards, Tony Romo's career is just starting. There will be more touchdowns, how-did-he-do-that? runs, and last-second wins. There will be more commericials, more ESPN spots, and probably more sightings with a celebrity blonde, brunette or two, or three.

Romo has not done everything, not by any standard. It took Peyton Manning nine years in the NFL before he won his first Super Bowl. John Elway played 15 seasons before he finally won his first title. Steve Young played in two leagues, and didn't win his first Super Bowl until he was 33.

But Romo's beginning as a starter suggests that it's not too far fetched to believe he, too, will win a Super Bowl, with the Cowboys. On October 30, 2007, Jerry Jones called off his search for the quarterback he longed for when he signed Romo to the type of contract he could never have imagined when he was a rookie. It was the type of contract that only the "franchise" quarterbacks sign: six years worth $67.5 million.

"This is a feel-good story," Jones said. "It's about an invidiual that wouldn't take no for an answer. I can't tell you I've ever sat beside anybody I felt better about because of how he got here."

Jones, Romo and the rest of the NFL had more than enough evidence to know Romo wasn't a strike of lightning. There was more than enough evidence to suggest that the ball didn't just find Romo's bat. In his first 16 games as a starting quarterback for the Cowboys, Romo would have shattered just about every single season passing record in franchise history.

The link between Dandy Don Meredith in the 1960s, Roger Staubach in the 1970s, Danny White in the 1980s and Troy Aikman in the 1990s is the kid from Burlington, Wisconsin who was never offered a full ride scholarship. "It feels like we've accomplished something, but it doesn't," Romo said the day he signed the contract. "It's the beginning of something."

The kid who went undrafted had officially beat out all of those Cowboys prospects with the "superior" credentials – Quincy Carter, Chad Hutchinson, Drew Henson, and finally Drew Bledsoe – to finally end Jerry Jones's search for The Man at quarterback.

For every high school kid who never thought he'd have a shot at a scholarship, even if it's only a partial offer, there is Tony Romo to prove one can be had. For every small college football player who longed for just one single shot to prove he could play in the biggest league the sport offers, there is Tony Romo to prove it can happen.

"No matter where you come from, you can do this or you can't," Romo said. "There is no secret. You have the ability or you don't. Just because you work hard doesn't necessarily guarantee you are going to have success. It gives you a better chance.

"Either you can perform at a consistently high level more often or you can't. That's why I think anyone from anywhere can be good."

Romo is not where he is today without his family. He's not where he is today without his father occasionally dropping the hammer, and not heaping mounds of unwarranted praise.

Romo is not where he is today if it weren't Burlington, and for high school coaches such as Bill Berkholtz, Hans Brock or Steve Brezowitz.

Romo is not where he is today without Eastern Illinois coach Roy Wittke convincing head coach Bob Spoo to give Romo that partial scholarship.

Romo is not where he is today without Cowboys scout Jim Hess convincing his team to look at him. Romo is not where he is today without Sean Payton and David Lee working with him. Romo is not where he is today without coach Bill Parcells patiently waiting for him to develop, and then putting him in when he thought Romo was ready.

For the "little guy" from the "little school" a lot of things had to go right, and a lot of people had to help.

But he is also good. The NFL doesn't play, and pay guys who simply work hard.

Has his fame changed him? Yep. You aren't invited to swishy L.A. parties because you're a nice guy. You don't suddenly start dating pop culture names such as Carrie Underwood or Sophia Bush because of a nice smile. His success for one of America's most popular sports franchises has opened doors to these places, and these people. But it doesn't change who he is.

Will the multi-million dollar contract change him? "I think I'm definitely a better person because I have more money," he joked. He has a hard time imagining what to buy. The contract is just the contract – it's a lot of money. More money doesn't guarantee anything except a bigger bank account and increased expectations for a football player. More money doesn't guarantee a Super Bowl which is where Romo desperately wants this story to include ... preferably in February of 2008.

Few can argue his success wasn't earned. And almost no one can argue that his story isn't inspiring. Romo is proof that you don't need to follow the prototypical story to be successful. That work, effort and a firm belief in yourself can carry you further than a great arm, big body or can't-miss-genetics.

"I absolutely love that guy. He's so confident," former Cowboys special teams coach Bruce DeHaven said of Romo. "The guy thinks he's the greatest thing since sliced bread ... and, hell, he's probably right." ■